MW00526746

The Seaweed Cookbook

XA MILNE

MICHAEL JOSEPH
an imprint of
PENGUIN BOOKS

MICHAEL JOSEPH

UK | USA | Canada | Ireland | Australia
India | New Zealand | South Africa

Michael Joseph is part of the Penguin Random House group of companies
whose addresses can be found at global.penguinrandomhouse.com.

First published by Michael Joseph 2016
001

Text copyright © Xa Milne, 2016

The moral right of the author has been asserted

Set in 10.4/15 pt Sabon LT Pro
Typeset by Jouve (UK), Milton Keynes
Printed in Great Britain by Clays Ltd, St Ives plc

A CIP catalogue record for this book is available from the British Library

ISBN: 978–0–718–183660

www.greenpenguin.co.uk

Penguin Random House is committed to a
sustainable future for our business, our readers
and our planet. This book is made from Forest
Stewardship Council® certified paper.

To Simon and my boys with love

CONTENTS

SEAWEED COOKBOOK

Orange wakame seaviche
Cured mackerel fillets
Spinach and toasted shony ricotta balls 🌿
Dulse popcorn with maple syrup 🌿
Elisabeth Luard's cheese shortbreads with dulse 🌿
Mooie's flatbread 🌿
Corn on the cob with dulse chilli and lime butter 🌿

MAINS 127

Rare beef with salsa verde and dulse slaw
White bean and sausage stew with dulse aioli
Crispy pork belly with fennel and kombu, apple chutney
    and aioli slaw in warm flatbreads
Michael Smith's breast of lamb with crisp kale and dulse
    crumbs
Lamb koftas with dulse
Get wrapped: Lamb in kombu
Duck breasts with seaweed seasoning
Cardamom chicken thighs with lemon and dulse
    yoghurt
Hugh's foil-baked fish with smoked dulse and garlic
Monkfish kebabs with sea lettuce
Grilled sea bass with tarragon, lemon and shony
Spaghetti vongole with kombu
Kedgeree with kombu
Cashew nut curry with kombu 🌿
Courgette with sumac-roasted cherry tomatoes 🌿
Lentil burgers with dulse 🌿
Spinach and goat's cheese frittata with dulse 🌿
Mushroom risotto with kombu and kale 🌿

PUDDINGS AND SWEET TREATS 155

Cashew nut and shony lemon cheesecake 🌿
Dulse banana ice cream 🌿
Shony chocolate and frozen 🌿
Damson cranachan 🌿

CONTENTS

xi

THE WORLD IS TOO MUCH WITH US

The world is too much with us; late and soon,
Getting and spending, we lay waste our powers;—
Little we see in Nature that is ours;
We have given our hearts away, a sordid boon!
This Sea that bares her bosom to the moon;
The winds that will be howling at all hours,
And are up-gathered now like sleeping flowers;
For this, for everything, we are out of tune;
It moves us not. Great God! I'd rather be
A Pagan suckled in a creed outworn;
So might I, standing on this pleasant lea,
Have glimpses that would make me less forlorn;
Have sight of Proteus rising from the sea;
Or hear old Triton blow his wreathèd horn.

William Wordsworth

INTRODUCTION

I see this book as a starter manual that hopefully goes some way to plug the knowledge gap between wanting to use seaweed and not knowing how to. Many of our friends, family and colleagues have genuinely enthused about and shared this passion for seaweed, the most ancient of foods, which seems more relevant today even than in the time of St Columba. However, they later confessed that the packets they had bought lay unopened or abandoned on the top shelf of a cupboard. Incorporating seaweed into your diet is not a test of endurance or a caveman challenge, quite the reverse. It is about enjoying an ingredient in an entirely natural and rational way, in keeping with modern eating habits.

In this book, I have created a range of dishes that benefit from this low-sodium, umami-laden food and that use various herbs, spices and ingredients to complement the different seaweeds. We often unwittingly use umami foods as the building blocks of what we choose to cook and seaweed is another such foundation food, but one that brings so much more to the party. It is not only a viable salt alternative, making your food taste better, but is also stacked with nutrients and phytochemicals. I have been on an incredible journey from learning about Spring Tides to Spring Rolls and through quite a lot in the middle. The love of seaweed has taught me to appreciate the work that goes into producing food on the plate. The fact that it can only be picked at the lowest tides at certain times of the month makes it an extraordinarily resilient food that is resistant to overpicking, not least because it is hidden in its mineral bath most of the time.

I love it for its ability to keep, even improve, its extraordinary flavour profile, even having been stored in a dark place for many months. It is incredible watching whole leaf seaweed turn to a ground pastel-coloured flake, powder or flour. The extreme saltiness of dried seaweed is as extraordinary as the mildness and neutrality of young fresh seaweed straight out of the sea. I also love the way it can be coaxed back to life when submerged in water and becomes a succulent sea vegetable ready to be chopped into soup. Most of all, I have been amazed by its ability to transform ordinary food into something really special.

I hope you enjoy it!

BEGINNINGS

Improbably, my passion for seaweed, or salvo, started with the Xbox and my boys' increasing disconnection from the outdoor world. This led to a journey with fellow school mum Fiona Houston, and our pack of assorted kids, searching for the ultimate wild edibles lying neglected in our hedgerows, beaches and copses. The end result was *Seaweed and Eat It: A Family Foraging and Cooking Adventure* (Virgin 2008).

What really excited me was discovering that some of these foods had once been part of British culture and history, and had simply been forgotten about. From sweetly scented Roman pot herbs like Alexanders (*Smyrnium olusatrum*), blooming on a Fife beach, to scurvy grass (*Cochlearia officinalis*) (a source of vitamin C for sailors on their long voyages) found near a bus stop in Edinburgh, all of these foods have a past and connect us to a time when life was simpler.

But it was seaweed that really made us stop and think. I knew our ancestors had eaten it in Mesolithic times and that it had been a vital famine food in Ireland and parts of the Hebrides. Today, it is a dietary staple in Southeast Asia. So why weren't we eating it?

While researching the book, we watched Margaret Horne, a smooth-skinned restaurateur, munch on a piece of Dulse picked freshly off the beach in Auchmithie on the Scottish East Coast, and I wondered why it had dropped off our list of go-to ingredients. Who would have guessed that a piece of seaweed plucked from under the lapping waves could have such a surprising taste. The flavour was much milder than I had imagined. As I chewed on the chestnut-purple blade, the delicate saltiness gave way to an almost nutty, meaty taste, which made me think of yeast extract, Marmite, bowls of comforting broth. It was strangely moreish, I was hooked.

I now know that the delicious taste I was experiencing was umami – the fifth taste. Remembered from breast milk and recognized by a taste receptor on the tip of your tongue, umami sends signals to the brain, triggering a taste receptor in the stomach that picks up on glutamates and readies itself for receiving protein and nourishment. How neat that a coding system exists in the hard wiring of the brain to ensure our well being.

Seaweed contains all 56 minerals and trace elements essential for optimum health. It also contains as much as 10 to 20 times the minerals of land plants and incorporating as little as a spoonful a day into your diet can therefore make a real difference.

SETTING UP THE BUSINESS

In 2011 Fiona Houston and I co-founded Mara Seaweed, with the intent to supply chefs and home cooks with a range of premium dried and ground seaweed seasonings from Scotland and Ireland. By that stage, we were confident that our seaweed product range would be well received. We had taste-tested seaweed samples with chefs in Edinburgh who were embracing new ways of introducing salt and flavour into food. The fact that seaweed comes in a form that is so easy to use was a plus point. The flavours were extraordinary and it also has a good shelf life: tick, tick, tick. Taste references ranged from nam pla fish sauce to piment d'Espelette in terms of its potential.

We had been to Ireland and watched harvesters picking barrel loads of new season Dulse, Kombu, Sea Lettuce and Pepper Dulse off the beach. The cold crashing Atlantic waves were just what was required to produce top-quality seaweed and Máirtín, the harvester, maintained just the right amount of artisanal cool. The harvest season ran from April to October and in the winter months he took off to New Zealand. It sounded like Máirtín had life well worked out. The seaweed would wait until he returned. The beauty of working with a seasonal product is that his work patterns were well established because they were dependent on the phases of the moon, when it was new or full.

Back in Scotland, the seaweed wave was building. Scottish Enterprise started to account manage and wind us into a programme of workshops, trade shows and events. We did new product development work with Abertay University, learning how to market and develop our products. We were fast tracked. We were being sat alongside whisky, shortbread, haggis and salmon retailers. We were a part of the Scottish diaspora peddling mountains, sea and fresh air. Through Scottish Development International (SDI), we found ourselves in Paris at a major European food trade show, SIAL, with a delegation from Scotland including kilted smoked salmon sellers, gluten-free bread and venison pâté makers. We were carded by Harrods Branded Pantry and a large US retail chain at the show, and told that they loved our branding and that we had an extraordinary range of products. This was the moment we knew we were on the right path. In an international marketplace our ancient product with new clothes on looked appealing. It looked modern, it looked like it had always been there. Harrods stocked us two years later and that was really where it began for Mara.

Our team of two grew when ex-marine lawyer and seaweed-lover Rory MacPhee, our Seaweed Harvester, joined us from Cornwall. This self-styled 'Maraman' arrived with his handmade curragh, his Leatherman knife and his can-do attitude. Mara Seaweed's first operations took place in Fife on a coastline that officially belongs to the Queen. Fiona (CEO) had been first in line to be granted a Crown Estate Licence in mainland Scotland, provided that we could initially survey the area to be harvested and provide detailed coordinates. I have an image of Tabitha, our graduate intern, out on the beach in her neoprene on a blustery day with her giant protractor and a back pack overflowing with seaweed, and the nonplussed expressions of the local dog walkers.

Rory brought passion and the love of harvesting to the party. He manages risk control balanced with the need to bring in as much seaweed as possible, sustainably and safely. Rory's rituals are based on respect and love of the environment. He can turn seaweed into food in the space of about two minutes, armed with only a bottle of soy sauce, some chopsticks and a sprinkle of chilli. He has style!

In 2012 Mara won money from a Government-funded project to investigate the viability of growing seaweed in onshore tanks on the West Coast of Scotland in partnership with a local business and the Scottish Association for Marine Science (SAMS). This tacked on nicely to a seaweed rope-growing operation of ours that was being trialled by Loch Fyne Oysters. We all saw the potential for growing it in a controlled environment and jobs for people in the outer fringes appealed to the Mara Mission. If it doesn't exist, create it. Rory and Fiona began to oversee all sorts of different projects to do with growing and harvesting, following on from countries where this already exists, like Norway and the Netherlands.

Back on the East Coast, seaweed harvesting was underway, with Sea Spice Cottage acting as our hub where seaweed is seasonally harvested before being taken to our HQ in Granton, Edinburgh, to be dried. The process is about as natural as it could possibly be within the stringent Food Safety Management Scheme and Hazard Analysis and Critical Control Plan (HACCP) required by the industry, along with acquiring SALSA (Safe and Local Supplier Accreditation). It is imperative to us that our seaweeds retain their extraordinary taste and flavour profile. We have produced something premium and Scottish in character, a million miles away from the intensive seaweed farming that occupies hundreds of hectares in the South China Sea.

Our team grew again and we gained a chairman and a production manager, as well as new premises in Granton. We looked out on the Firth of Forth and beyond to the North Sea.

Our break came when we were championed by Sheila Dillon from Radio 4's *The Food Programme* and nominated in the Best Local Food Producer category in the Food and Farming Awards 2015, in which we were runners up. Simultaneously one of our products, Dulse, hit the shelves in M&S. They had got it, hallelujah.

While chefs are still really important, we were trying to appeal to the everyday cook. It was always the plan to make life simpler, not harder. A little sprinkle of seaweed to add flavour and health and stir something magic into your pot to nourish and warm you.

SURVIVAL FOOD

Seaweed, or marine algae, is to fish and the marine environment what fungi are to trees and plants: together they create a healthy and balanced ecosystem. Algae have been growing in our oceans for millennia, oxygenating the sea before man walked the earth. There is evidence that seaweed was a survival food in Europe since the time of Mesolithic man, along with marine molluscs, fish, sea birds, sea and wild land mammals.[1]

In the seventh century, St Columba describes in a poem the ideal life of the ascetic monk and talks of him 'cropping Dulse from the rock'. Dulse was eaten with oatmeal in a thick mealy broth or served boiled and softened with butter. The monks on Iona collected it to provide food for themselves and for the poor. This was known as 'Dulsing'.

Fergus Kelly's book on land values tells us that the value of a rock covered with Dulse was equal to that of a cow.[2] 'Bo are charraigh thoraigh dia mbentar duileasg no femnach', or 'A cow for a productive rock, from which Dulse is cut'. You were considered a rich man if you possessed any of the following: 'garlic, salt or Dulse'.

Food historian Catherine Brown observes that there are twenty-two different Gaelic names for seaweeds, suggesting that they were an everyday part of the Scottish diet.[3]

Seaweed was all-important as a survival food in Scotland between 1790–1820, when crofters were sent to coastal dwellings to make way for sheep. It was routinely collected from the shore and dug into the soil as fertilizer, providing high levels of potassium and nitrogen. Lazy bed cultivation became commonplace, where wide trenches were dug and seaweed thrown up by winter storms was laid on the earth piles for several weeks before being turned back into the trenches where they would plant their root crops. On every headland where Wrack seaweed used to come, libations of bowls of porridge were frequently thrown to the God of the Sea, 'Shony', in the hope that he would return the favour (see prayer below). One of the earliest accounts of this ceremony, written about by Martin Martin in 1695, was undertaken by the church of St Moluag on the Isle of Lewis where every family was given a peck of malt, which was then brewed into ale. One of the congregation was then chosen to wade into the sea at shallow tide on the evening of 31 October, the beginning of winter, and offer up their cup of ale in the hope that, in return, they would be sent plenty of sea ware (seaweed).

In Ireland it became part of the diet during the potato famine after 1846 and in Scotland, as many as 40,000 folk depended on seaweed for their livelihood between the seventeenth and early nineteenth centuries, when Kelp burning was at its peak. The alkaline potash by-product of this process was used in glazing and glass making.

Ortha Feamainn (Prayer for Seaweed)[4]

A prayer from the people of the Western Isles hoping that prolonged periods of calm give way to westerly winds, which bring seaweed in to shore, to stave off impending famine.

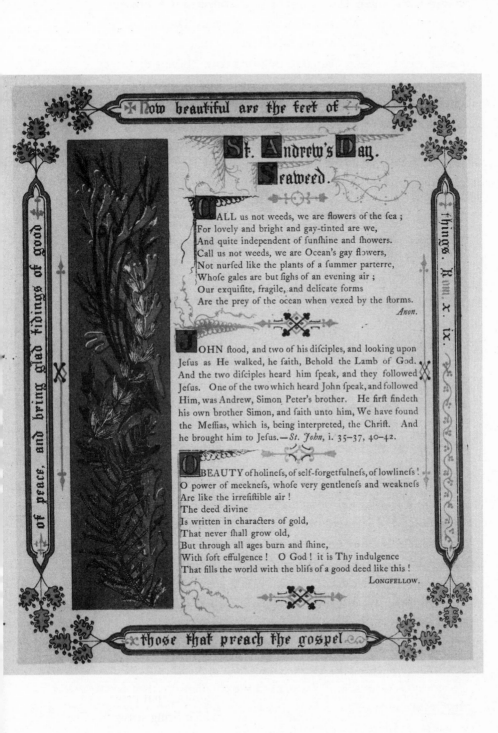

St. Andrew's Day.
Seaweed.

CALL us not weeds, we are flowers of the sea;
For lovely and bright and gay-tinted are we,
And quite independent of sunshine and showers.
Call us not weeds, we are Ocean's gay flowers,
Not nursed like the plants of a summer parterre,
Whose gales are but sighs of an evening air;
Our exquisite, fragile, and delicate forms
Are the prey of the ocean when vexed by the storms.

Anon.

JOHN stood, and two of his disciples, and looking upon
Jesus as He walked, he saith, Behold the Lamb of God.
And the two disciples heard him speak, and they followed
Jesus. One of the two which heard John speak, and followed
Him, was Andrew, Simon Peter's brother. He first findeth
his own brother Simon, and saith unto him, We have found
the Messias, which is, being interpreted, the Christ. And
he brought him to Jesus.—*St. John,* i. 35-37, 40-42.

O BEAUTY of holiness, of self-forgetfulness, of lowliness!
O power of meekness, whose very gentleness and weakness
Are like the irresistible air!
The deed divine
Is written in characters of gold,
That never shall grow old,
But through all ages burn and shine,
With soft effulgence! O God! it is Thy indulgence
That fills the world with the bliss of a good deed like this!

LONGFELLOW.

Toradh mara gu tìr,	*Produce of sea to land,*
Toradh tìre gu muir;	*Produce of land to sea;*
Neach nach dèan 'na ìr,	*He who doeth not in time,*
Crìon gum bi a chuid.	*Scant shall his share be.*
Feamainn 'ga cur gu tìr,	*Seaweed being cast on shore*
Builich, a Thì na buil;	*Bestow, Thou Being of bestowal;*
Toradh 'ga chur an nì,	*Produce being brought to wealth,*
A Chriosda, thoir mo chuid!	*O Christ, grant me my share!*

Foghnadh Feamainn (Abundance of Seaweed)

A prayer from the people of the Western Isles rejoicing and singing hymns of praise to the gracious God of the Sea who has heard their prayers.

Thàine 's gun tàine feamainn,	*Come and come is seaweed,*
Thàine 's gun tàine brùchd,	*Come and come is red sea ware,*
Thàine buidheag 's thàine lighag,	*Come is yellow weed, come is tangle,*
Thàine biadh mu 'n iadh an stùc.	*Come is food which the wave enwraps.*
Thàinig Mìcheal mìl na conail,	*Come is Michael of fruitage,*
Thàinig Brighde bhìth na ciùin,	*Come is womanly Brigit of gentleness,*
Thàinig a' Mhathair mhìn Mhoire,	*Come is the mild Mother Mary,*
'S thàinig Connan àigh an iùil.	*And come is glorious Connan of guidance.*

ANCIENT FOOD TO BILLION POUND INDUSTRY

An early nineteenth-century etching by Walter Geikie depicts a typical street scene in Edinburgh of a vendor selling 'bawbee pooches' (halfpenny pouches) of 'crisp saline' Dulse or 'Tangle' (Alaria) out of wicker creels. Today on the North and East Coasts of Scotland, Dulse is still roasted on embers, sprinkled with vinegar and eaten as a snack, and purple Laver (Porphyra or Nori) is still eaten in Wales as a component of Laverbread.

British phycologist Kathleen Mary Drew-Baker, 'Mother of the Sea', rescued the Japanese Nori industry in 1948 after a series of typhoons hit Japan, which, combined with polluted waters, resulted in the collapse of Nori production. No one could work out how to grow Nori from scratch. Drew-Baker, with her knowledge of the different growing cycles of Porphyra, published a paper in 1949 that precipitated artificial methods of growing seedlings, and the saving of the entire industry in Japan. Nori is now a billion pound industry. It is sold all over the world as one of the most prized seaweeds and has become the ultimate low-calorie snack.

TODAY

Seaweed is like Marmite – there are people who love it and those who have yet to convert. There is a growing trend for innovative chefs to include seaweed in their menus, from René Redzepi at Noma and his team at the Nordic Food Lab to Nathan Outlaw and Brett Graham at the Ledbury and Heston Blumenthal. What all these chefs share is the belief that the fifth taste, umami, is a crucial factor in our enjoyment of food.

Lack of pleasure from food, or lack of taste, often results in poor diet and subsequent health issues. Clinical tests[5] have revealed that umami taste stimulation can increase the salivary flow, which is particularly pertinent for the elderly where taste receptors can often be impaired. Umami in food thus promotes palatability.

There is an ongoing, global shift in attitude towards food that increasingly calls for natural and ethically sourced ingredients as part of a healthy, well-balanced diet. In the global marketplace, the presence of products that have a positive and tangible impact on your health, such as seaweed, has increased by 85% in the past 10 years.[6]

Cybercolloids Ltd, an Irish-based company who research and develop products specialising in hydrocolloids, recently researched[7] the flavour and taste of seaweed using a tasting panel to assess its potential as a commercial product. Wakame (Alaria), Kombu, Sugar kelp, Sea spaghetti, Dulse and Sea lettuce were all considered as contenders to be sold as dry savoury ingredients and condiments. The outcome of the research project was positive in terms of the future application of seaweed in the food industry, with successes ranging from salts through to dry and wet condiments, soups, sauces, marinades, baked products, savoury products and drinks. The report[8] concluded that seaweed is an underexploited, naturally nutritious 'superfood'.

Sheffield Hallam University[9] presents epidemiological evidence that regular seaweed consumption may protect us against various modern diseases as well as enhancing satiety, increasing food acceptability and improving the shelf-life of foods. When 5g of seaweed, instead of salt, is added to bakery products, particularly wholemeal bread, there is no mould growth for up to nine days in their control sample. What seems clear is that seaweed has a place in the modern diet and food applications.

TASTE

Umami exists in amniotic fluid, so we all taste it before we even enter this world. In effect, we understand about the five taste modalities from the word go, and there is nothing like a child's facial expressions to indicate whether they are experiencing sweet, sour, salt, bitter or umami (extra big grin). The reason for the umami smile is that umami-rich food (seaweed being the richest source) contains glutamates and is associated with comfort.

The words most commonly used by chefs all around the world to explain umami are balance and depth. They fully understand the benefits of having umami in their cooking. Umami draws the flavour out of ingredients without having to use strong seasoning. A strange shift of the palate happens where you do not need as much salt or sugar to make your food taste good.

As recently as forty years ago, umami was almost an unknown concept. Chef Alexandre Bourdas explains it as 'bringing pleasure to the palate'.[10] This sensation starts at the back of the mouth and ends up in the nose, resulting in the eater wanting more. This rich savouriness lends good 'mouth-feel' to our experience.

In 1908, Japanese chemist Dr Kikunae Ikeda first isolated MSG in Kombu and came up with the word 'umami', meaning savoury deliciousness, and went on to develop the concept of the fifth taste. Kombu has more natural MSG than any other raw, organic material. As well as high amounts of MSG, there are other amino acids that impart a sweet taste to the seaweed. Professor Ole Mouritsen, a gastronomist who works as an academic in Denmark and is attached to the Nordic Food Lab, describes Dashi stock (made from Kombu) as having 'sweet and floral notes'. Gastronomic food tests with Dulse proved that it was a better source of umami agents than Japanese Kombu in terms of alaninate, which contributes to its mild sweet taste. Their tests using Dulse dashi to infuse fresh cheese, ice cream and sourdough with Dulse extract illustrated that Dulse is a very successful flavouring agent and 'holds a great promise for novel uses not only in the New Nordic Cuisine, but in general'.[11] Often we are eating umami-rich food and we don't even know it, for example in Parmesan and tomatoes. We are often drawn to it without being aware of why we are reaching for the sauce bottle or the cheese grater.

Umami is made up of glutamates, inosinates and guanylates. Experienced together, the taste impact is greater. For example, Kombu with tuna, onion, carrot, celery and beef, or spring onion, ginger and chicken, brings out the best flavour profile in each ingredient. This is called umami synergy. Tests have proved that the ideal ratio of glutamate to inosinate is 1:1, which intensifies the flavour by roughly 7 or 8 times what it would normally be.[12]

THE TRUTH ABOUT SALT

Salt reduction is a crucial consideration in the food industry today and natural non-sodium alternatives are being sought. 1g of table salt (NaCl) contains 0.4g of sodium, whereas 1g of (Irish) seaweed contains between 0.025g to 0.047g sodium, depending on species and locality. In other words, seaweed contains about eight times less sodium than salt, as well as providing potassium, magnesium, calcium, iron and iodine.

The World Health Organisation has recognized that salt reduction is as important to our health as stopping smoking is for heart disease. A high salt diet can contribute to obesity, stomach cancer, kidney disease, strokes and heart attacks. Kay Diley, nutritionist at Consensus Action Salt and Health (CASH), believes that 75% of the salt we eat is hidden in the food we buy and most of us are eating more than the recommended dose of 6g per day (about a teaspoon),[13] bread still being one of the largest contributors of salt in our diets.

Contrary to popular myth, gourmet salts are no better than table salts – they just cost a lot more – containing on average 98% sodium chloride (versus on average 10% sodium chloride in dried seaweed) and no added health benefits or minerals. The consensus of the report is that we should flavour our food with spices, herbs and other natural seasonings. Seaweed can be used as a natural flavour enhancer, preservative, and can, when used in home cooking, help reduce the amount of table salt required. Move over sea salt, hello seaweed.

When you consume more umami, the improved flavour means that fewer calories and less salt are required for a satisfying taste experience. The Hotchkiss study concluded that Alaria and Dulse offered the greatest potential (in dry and wet applications), and were deemed to improve flavour with their pleasant characteristics and saltiness. Including seaweed in foods has been shown to have a preservative effect, producing less bacteria,[14] thus reducing the need to add salt.

WHERE SEAWEED GROWS

There are approximately 10,000 edible seaweeds around the world from Australia to the East Coast of America. Many of the same seaweeds that grow in Asia and North America are native to the UK and are found in abundance around our 11,000km of coastline, including the most widely eaten: Nori, Wakame and Kombu. Their taste ranges from peppery to sweet, through smoky and herby. Like land vegetables, they have different growing seasons, different growing conditions and maintain unique flavour and nutrient profiles.

WHAT DO THEY LOOK LIKE?
BROWN SEAWEEDS (KELPS) (PHAEPHYTA)

Kelp seaweeds are found in the deep water and are best picked at the lowest spring tides – January to June is the optimum time. They contain more vitamins, minerals and trace elements than any other food on earth and are excellent mineral supplements. They are high in soluble fibre and iodine, which help thyroid function and fertility, and are an excellent low-calorie, high-energy food source.

Kombu *Laminaria digitata*
(Oarweed, Sea tangle, Sea ribbon)

Brown in colour with long leather straps, like a giant palm with finger-like fronds.

Kombu tastes surprisingly sweet, herby, salty, olivey and earthy. In cookery, the primary function of Kombu seaweeds is to lend a base flavour to stocks (dashi).

Healthwise, Kombu is iodine-rich and high in naturally occurring sugars, potassium and sodium in the right proportions for healthy cell function. A great source of energy.

Wakame *Alaria esculenta*
(Tangle, Murlin, Henware, Dabberlocks, Wing kelp, Honeyware)

This seaweed is easily recognizable as the one that you fish out of a bowl of miso soup. It is dark brown or green and can grow up to 2 metres in length. Alaria has a mild, sweet taste and when eaten young enough, the juicy midribs taste a bit like radish tops.

Healthwise, Alaria is rich in osteoporosis-preventing calcium (it has 10 times the amount of calcium as milk) and is loaded with magnesium and particularly iodine.

Sea spaghetti *Himanthalia elongata*
(Thong weed, Button weed, Sea bean, Sea haricots, Sea thong)

This type of seaweed is really easy to spot as it looks like strands of tagliatelle growing from a little rubbery sucker. When picking, take a few fronds from each button only.

Sea spaghetti has a mild taste and is therefore a brilliant carrier for other flavours in food. It has a sweetness, so works well being candied, ceviched in lemon juice or mixed in with land pasta. Like other varieties of kelp, it is rich in iodine, calcium, magnesium and potassium.

Sugar wrack *Saccharina latissima*
(Sugar kelp, Poor man's weather glass, Sea belt)

This seaweed is an easy one to find on the beach. Look for large brown fronds of blistered seaweed, crinkly and undulating, sometimes as long as 4 metres in length.

Sugar wrack is salty when roasted, with a taste reminiscent of bacon. Rich in calcium, iodine and magnesium, it's good in seaweed crisps or dried and powdered and put into soups and stews.

Bladderwrack *Fucus vesiculosus*
(Rockweed, Sea wrack)

Easy to identify with its forked, wavy-edged fronds and popping bladders, often in pairs, Bladderwrack starts off an olive/brown colour and darkens as it ages. It grows up to 50cm in length and you're likely to slip on it whilst clambering over rocks. When gathering, pick only a few fronds from each plant.

Young Bladderwrack buds have a delicate flavour and are great for putting into salads. With its antiviral properties, this is also an excellent seaweed to dry and use as an infusion.

Channel wrack *Pelvetia canaliculata*
(Cow tang)

This small wrack is olive-green to brown, with curved or channelled sides to its fronds and grows in bunch-like formations, often found on rocks high up on the shoreline. It has a light, saline flavour which could be the base for a power drink or turbo-charged tea.

Knotted wrack *(Ascophyllum nodosum)*
(Yellow tang, Sea whistle)

Olive-green to yellow seaweed with egg-shaped sacs at intervals along long, slim fronds. This seaweed is harvested in the Hebrides and used commonly as a food supplement or nutraceutical. Mild, salty flavour. Anti-coagulant, anti-thrombotic and anti-inflammatory properties. Dried and crumbled, it is perfect for adding to drinks or soups.

RED SEAWEEDS (RHODOPHYTA)

This group is found between the low intertidal zone and deep water. These seaweeds are commonly eaten in the UK, North America and Canada, as well as in parts of Scandinavia and Europe. Their distinctive colour pigment helps absorb the limited sunrays that are able to penetrate at this depth. As they are primarily composed of carbohydrates and are rich in iron, red seaweeds are a good source of energy. Red marine algae, in particular, contains powerful antiviral agents.

Dulse *Palmaria palmata*
(Dillisk, Creathnach)

The Dulse leaf starts off greenish yellow and becomes dark brownish-red with purple tones which become richer as the season advances. It varies in size, from a single broad blade to narrow segments, delicate and fine, with rounded ends. Dulse leaves are often attached by their holdfast onto larger kelps or rocks, frequently hidden by overhangs of more commonly found wracks.

The taste of Dulse is very distinctive: umami in spades, with nutty, liquorice, meaty flavour notes becoming more smoky and salty as it dries. When it is fried, it tastes almost of bacon, and it makes a less salty alternative to anchovies in cooking. Icelandic Chef Aggi Sverrisson confessed on BBC's *Saturday Kitchen* that he sprinkles dried ground Dulse (Sol) on all of his white fish and in most of the desserts that he cooks.

Iron-rich and incorporating all the trace elements, Dulse's minerals are roughly 10 times those of land vegetables. It is also an excellent source of iodine and very low in fat. It is a perfect combination of bio-available nutrients with five times more potassium than pistachios weight for weight. A good source of protein and fibre.

Pepper Dulse *Osmundea pinnatifida*
(Truffle of the sea)

This is the baby of the group, but with the most clout. It has fan-like frond arrangements, which are purplish-brown to black in colour, and prefers rocky crevices where it isn't exposed to light. You would find it in most places where mussels grow. It is labour-intensive to pick and hard to find, so this extraordinary truffle-tasting plant will never be widely available to buy. To harvest, cut halfway down the stem with small scissors, making sure that you only take a little from each clump.

The unique, piquant taste of Pepper Dulse (possibly caused by molecules called terpenese) which has chefs crying out for more, has been compared to truffles, with garlic and black pepper notes. When eaten fresh there is a herby, almost olivey taste, with an aftertaste of garlic. Dried or fresh, this seaweed goes well with scrambled eggs or hollandaise sauce and, when added to butter, makes the perfect finale to a cooked lobster. It is also a powerful antiviral agent.

Nori *Porphyra umbilicalis*
(Slake, Sloke, Slacan, Black butter, Purple sea vegetable, Laver, Karango, Sea leaf)

This seaweed, which has the highest value, on a global level, grows from mid to low shore, on large boulders or rocks. The best way to identify it is to look for something similar to melted bin bags on the rocks! When picking, take a little from each rock, so that it can regenerate. The colour can be olive-green to purple-brown or even black in appearance.

Nori's nutty, salty taste will be familiar to anyone who has had sushi (Nori rolls).

Healthwise, it has the highest protein content of all the seaweeds, is high in vitamin C, betacarotene and vitamin B12 amongst others. It contains lignin compounds and antioxidants, all of which have cancer-fighting properties.

Carragheen *Chondrus crispus*
(Irish moss, Dorset moss, Iberian moss, Carragheen moss, Pearl moss, Jelly moss)

A dark red to pink seaweed, fan-shaped with small spiked, rubbery, fronds. Often found growing beneath Kelp, it favours the middle or lower shore and can be found in and around rock pools.

Traditionally a food for invalids, boiled in milk with sugar or jam added, it is known for strengthening the respiratory tract and is gentle on your gut. Adds a delicate hint of ocean taste to puddings and drinks. Produces large amounts of sulfated polysaccharides with anti-viral properties.

GREEN SEAWEEDS (CHLOROPHYTA)

Most of this group grow in warm and shallow waters. Their distinctive colour comes from the chlorophylls, which mark these seaweeds as most closely resembling land plants. These are the easiest to find, emerald green marking them out from the grey of the rocks and the more muted colours of the other seaweeds.

Sea lettuce *Ulva lactuca*
(Chicory, Green laver, Lettuce)

Often to be found in rock pools on the beach, when young it is small and pale green, but as the season advances it gets darker. Cut two thirds of the way down the leaf and pick as you would cut-and-come-again lettuce; it is a thinning operation, not total removal.

This seaweed has a crisp saline taste, moving through the slight bitterness of chicory to spinach. As the seaweed matures, it develops a slightly metallic aftertaste. Crumble over fish or seafood, in bread or mousses, or it also works well shallow-fried for a few seconds or pickled.

Rich in iron, protein, calcium, manganese, potassium, silica and vitamins A, B and C. Particularly high in vitamin B12: one serving provides a large portion of your daily recommended intake.

Enteromorpha Intestinalis
(Sea grass, Gut weed, Ulva compressa)

It looks transparent, pale green, tubular, with crinkly fronds. It is small and grows in thick clumps on rocky shores, rock pools and large stones up to the high tide mark. Best in spring and summer. Gently cut with scissors three quartes of the way down the fronds, taking only enough for personal use. This is some people's favourite seaweed. It is easy to dry and can be crumbled and kept in a jar for use on seafood or fish, pasta, risottos and soups. It works well as a beautiful grass-green salt seasoning. Rich in iron and magnesium.

HARVESTING

There are half a dozen seaweed harvesters in the UK. Crown Estate owns most of the seabed, as far as the twelve nautical mile mark, and half the foreshore in the UK, and permission must be sought in order to harvest commercially. The foreshore extends from the high and low tide water marks of ordinary spring tides. The rest of the coastline is owned by private individuals or has been leased back to businesses or local authorities. Access rights to the beach need to be established with the landowner, and a harvesting licence obtained, if picking commercially.

In terms of how seaweed is harvested, like land vegetables, seaweed has distinct seasons. The prime harvesting times are between April and October, with Nori and Pepper Dulse growing throughout the winter. The nutritional value changes according to what part of the growing season you are in.

Even before seasonality, it is necessary to note the phases of the moon. Tides are caused by the gravitational pull of the moon and the sun on the earth. When the moon, earth and sun align, as takes place during new and full moons, the sun's gravity adds to the moon's gravity and can make the high tide bulges even larger, which makes the low tides even lower. These two days each month when the tides are at their most extreme are called spring tides. Roughly there are about 12 days a month when the tides are low enough to harvest.

Harvesters are subject to rigorous safety management where a certain protocol has to be observed and adhered to. First, the stretch of coastline is scoped out and the Crown Estate Licence (supported by Scottish Natural Heritage) granted. The beaches where Mara harvests are rotated seasonally and sustainably. Each seaweed has its own unique growth cycle and is only cut when it is not breeding. Wild stocks are gathered from below Mean Low Water Spring Tide Mark. No seaweed is gathered from the foreshore and seaweed is never gathered at Neap Tides, that is when there is no moon.

Water quality is constantly monitored by environmental agencies in the UK, which you can find out by going online for the individual ratings of specific beaches.

Seaweed is harvested from only the cleanest possible marine environments, supported by the Environmental Agency (EA) in England and the Scottish Environmental Protection Agency (SEPA) in Scotland. Mara analyses all harvested seaweed in United Kingdom Accreditation Service (UKAS)-approved laboratories, where it is routinely tested for heavy metals, micro-biological contamination and nutrients, and anything that is harvested is subject to traceability. This is Mara's standard practice resulting in premium food-grade seaweed.

Pickers assemble on the shore at least two hours before low tide and put on high vis jackets, non-slip shoes and even buoyancy aids if they are picking in the sub-tidal zone. The harvesting window is until roughly 1 hour after low tide. Pickers can use hands or tools, whatever the manager thinks is more effective. The main thing is to pick three quarters of the way down the stipe (stem) and to thin rather than take all. Pick the younger, healthy looking leaves. You must never keep your back towards the tide!

Maraman Rory treats the sea and what comes out of it with the utmost respect. All his harvesters are deeply connected to bio-dynamic rhythms and start the day off with this evocative incantation:

> May the glory of the earth be yours
> May the glory of the sea be yours
> May the glory of the sky be yours
> and may the glory of the heavens be yours.

DRYING

For those who want to bring some seaweed back to the kitchen after a foray onto the beach, it is very simple to process:

Rinse your seaweed thoroughly (at least four or five times) in a bucket or sink in fresh water, making sure that there are no barnacles or molluscs on the leaves (not dissimilar to cleaning garden vegetables).

Remove any parts of the plant that are poor quality or discoloured, then lay the clean leaves out on a large baking rack or tray.

If using fresh, your seaweed can be processed much like land vegetables and steamed or puréed and turned into a relish or soup. If you want to store your seaweed for future usage you can freeze or dry.

Place in an oven preheated to 100°F/Gas ¼ and dry overnight to retain a 'raw product' where the seaweed keeps its nutrient profile or, if you want to dry the leaf quickly, put in a hot oven at 180°F/Gas 4 for 15 to 20 minutes, checking to see that it doesn't burn.

Note: Kombu will take the longest because it is the most fibrous. Sea lettuce and Nori will dry in a matter of hours in a warm place. Dulse may need a bit longer.

Either crumble the dried seaweed into a jar or whizz up in a coffee grinder. You can store your dried seaweed in Kilner jars or containers. It will keep, if sealed and in a dark place, for at least a year.

SHORT FOOD CHAINS – THE FUTURE OF SEAWEED?

Seaweed as a resource in the UK is currently available through a handful of small artisan producers who harvest top-quality seaweed from our Atlantic and North Sea coastlines. If we are to grow our local food economy in the UK, with seaweed producers as part of the wider food system, we need to support small producers to sell through local markets and independent retailers as well as through the wider channels. This will enable consumers to have better access to healthier, fresher and less processed foods. The quality and provenance of local food (food with a story behind it) is undeniable, but most importantly it links us with our natural and social environment. It is back to seaweed fulfilling an increasingly important role, where meat production and cereal imports in the global north have created a huge imbalance in the global south. It could be time now to redress the balance, with seaweed playing a greater role in our diets and our overall health.

SEAWEED IN THE KITCHEN

A good way to start using seaweed in your everyday food is to begin combining it with ordinary land herbs, spices and ingredients. By integrating seaweed into oils, butters, pastes, stocks, rubs, marinades, salts, toppings, seasonings, purées, sauces and infusions an armoury of seaweed flavours can be built up, which can in turn boost dishes with the minimum of effort. This is just a starting point and will allow you to experiment freely and find many more ways to wind it into your diet.

Fresh seaweed

Young tender seaweed blades picked at low tide, rinsed and chopped and added to salads, dips, or even sautéed in a little oil and butter, are succulent and mild tasting. As the growing season progresses the flavour deepens, but there is hardly a greater treat than delicate fronds of new season seaweed incorporated into butters and oils to accompany grilled seafood or a piece of white fish. The garlicky, truffley notes of Pepper Dulse eaten on its own are an eating experience on a par with new season chanterelles or truffles. The verdant green of fresh Sea lettuce is begging to be mixed into pestos and muddled up with salad leaves and herbs with tangy dressings. Even something as simple as finely chopped Dulse or Kombu dipped in tamari and ginger dressing is a wonderful side dish which may well be the best thing you have ever tasted. This is umami magic working on a very subtle level.

Dried seaweed

Whole leaf rehydration does not take long. Don't be put off by a knotted clump of dried seaweed that looks a bit like leather straps (Kombu), or liquorice laces (Sea spaghetti), sitting on your counter top. In 5 minutes, much like a Chinese paper flower, it will have opened out and expanded and, once chopped, can be mixed in with onions, tomatoes, mushrooms, leeks and land herbs to create unique flavours and tastes. For added nutrients you can use the water you have soaked the seaweed in, just don't soak it too long as all the iodine will leach out. You would be surprised how easily Sea spaghetti blends into stir-fries and pasta dishes and whole leaf Dulse and Alaria mix in with soups, stews, salads and casseroles. The key is to balance big flavours and textures, but the whole will be so much more.

Seaweed flakes

For the time-pressed, dried seaweed flakes and sexy, super-charged dusts or powders, are perfect to have sitting by the cooker. They have a much more concentrated flavour, so you need much less than the fresh equivalent in your cooking to get results.

Dulse

Umami-rich, use where you would normally use anchovy to season red meat, such as in burgers, lasagne, mince and roasts, as well as game, salmon, tuna, gratins, roast vegetables, dips, spreads, unsalty cheese, toppings, mayonnaises, baking, soups and with dark chocolate.

Kombu

Stocks, white meat (chicken, pork), mushrooms, smoothies, baking, seafood dishes, asparagus, nuts and lentils.

Shony

This blend adds salty and sweet dimensions to grains, rice, sweet puddings, oatmeal, stir-fries and salads.

Cooking with seaweed is a guaranteed way to use less salt in cooking and on the table. Whether it is to season meat alongside land herbs and spices, swapping salt for seaweed in baking, or using seaweed as a topping on rice and pasta, it is a way of getting flavour into food without the high sodium levels.

Sea lettuce

Crumbled into vegetable soups, seafood and fish dishes; its wonderful salt-mineral taste really adds punch to plain, subtle foods. It works well in breads or savoury pastries too.

Nori

The most valued seaweed, globally speaking, it works really well mixed with salad vegetables such as cucumber, avocado, tomato, celery. Great in salts and rubs and scattered over smoked salmon or cured fish with a twist of lemon. This seaweed has a subtle but satisfying taste that deepens during chewing. One of the most user-friendly seaweeds. Can be incorporated into a variety of salads and rice dishes for taste and health.

Seaweed store cupboard

These are all ingredients that work well with umami seaweed. Some are ordinary ingredients and others are specialist, but most are widely available.

FRESH	DRY	
Parmesan	Sea salt	Fennel seeds
Lemons	Tinned or dried chickpeas	Dried rosemary
Limes	Cannellini or butter beans	Dijon mustard
Oranges	Lentils (Puy or Black Beluga)	Sweet chilli sauce
Tomatoes	Basmati rice	Vanilla pods
Fresh garlic	Gram (gluten-free) flour	Tabasco
Fresh ginger	Pearl barley	Horseradish
Spring onions	Quinoa	Gherkins
Honey	Arborio rice	Capers
Almond milk	Passata	Brown rice miso paste
Fresh mushrooms	Tomato purée	Soy sauce (Tamari)
Dark kale	Toasted sesame oil	Mirin
Chillies – red and	Groundnut oil	Unsalted almonds
green	Coconut oil	Ground almonds
Peppers	Red wine vinegar	Cashews
Fresh coconut	Maple syrup	Pistachios
Medjool dates	Green tea	Walnuts
Parsley	Matcha (Japanese green tea	Pecans
Thyme	powder)	Macadamia nuts
Tarragon	Maca powder (supplement, to	Tahini
Mint	balance and revitalize energy)	Sesame seeds
Coriander	Pomegranate molasses	Dried apricots
Lovage	Ground ginger	Goji berries
Basil	Cumin	Dessicated coconut
	Mustard seeds	Dried mushrooms
	Chilli flakes	(shitake, porcini)
	Cayenne pepper	Coconut cream
	Allspice	Molasses
	Sumac	Oatmeal
	Ground cinnamon/Cinnamon	Rolled oats
	sticks	Chia seeds
	Coriander seeds	White chocolate
	Peppercorns	Dark chocolate
	Cardamom seeds	Raw cacao powder
	Nutmeg	Dried yeast

Kombu, Dulse, Nori, Parmesan,
cooked tomatoes, spring onions, onions, celery,
beets, mushrooms, peas, asparagus, leeks, green tea,
squid, sea bream, cod, prawns, oysters, clams, scallops, mussels,
cheese, truffles, soy beans, potatoes, sweet potatoes,
Chinese cabbage, carrots, oyster sauce, eggs,
cured ham, sardines, mackerel, tuna, pork, bonito flakes,
beef, chicken, shrimps, dried porcini,
dried morels, dried shitake

SEAWEED TASTE NOTES

What does this seaweed taste like?

To get into the right mind set for new tastes you have to imagine a world with no flavour, where bland prevails and dull dominates. No spicy salt notes of liquorice, creamy sweetness of oysters, dry muskiness of truffles or the infinite pleasures of dark chocolate with its bitter sweet taste balance. No briny salt burst of olives or piercing sharpness of citrus.

Love it? Hate it? Adore it? The seaweed will take you back in time as the umami glutamates first experienced in the womb start penetrating your senses . . . something familiar, but an altogether new food group. Life will never be quite the same again. Open your gullet, wake up your taste buds and embrace something not quite remembered but as familiar as the maternal heartbeat.

Dulse

Salt notes give way to sweet with a deeply satisfying Marmitey, anchovy warmth as the flavour develops. There is a moreish quality to this seaweed, which unaccountably has you reaching into the pot for more.

Fresh whole leaf
Nutty, giving way to a meaty, savoury aftertaste.

Dried whole leaf
Liquoricey, salty, savoury.

Dried flaked
Anchovy, salty, sweet aftertaste.

Smoked Dulse

A marine equivalent of smoked paprika or smoked pepper, a special condiment prized by chefs, particularly in fine powder form. Just a little peck or pinch of this insanely beautiful purple powder adds exotic smokiness and smoulder to your aioli, mayonnaise, fish dishes, soups, curries or risotto dishes. Prized Dulse is slow-smoked over sweet, scented apple wood. The taste of sweet cured bacon is not a million miles away, but this is just as addictive. For vegetarians this is a useful flavour boost that gives vegetable matter a gentle kick, because sometimes it needs it!

Kombu

Fresh
Tough and fibrous. Better eaten cooked.

Dried flaked
Mild to taste, granular texture, with a green grass earthiness that adds a level of salt and herbiness to dishes. Rich in natural sugars, there is an underlying sweetness to this seaweed.

Powder or Dust
Both sweet and salt at the same time, with a hint of the ocean. Melts on your tongue, giving you a quick umami hit.

Alaria/Wakame

Fresh/Dried
Gentle, savoury, satisfying flavour notes, which develop on chewing. Generally it takes on the flavour of other ingredients that it is put with. A

perfect carrier, but also imparts delicate salt flavour. Leaves infused in marinades are soft to bite, and sit on the flavour fence between mineral and vegetable.

Nori/Laver

Dried

This is the taste of seaweed as a lot of people know it. The Nori roll outside wrapping beloved of sushi enthusiasts and the melt-on-the-tongue Nori sheets that represent a salt tingle and virtually no calories.

The level of marine flavour here is subtle, like the delicate sea flavour of a freshly sautéed scallop or pan-fried baby squid. This is a taste that doesn't linger; it delivers a gentle hit of marine flavour with the merest hint of brine.

Sea Lettuce *Ulva lactuca*

It is hard not to eat with your eyes here. The colour of Sea lettuce makes you think of pea shoots, new beech leaves, lime zest and mown grass. This seaweed loves sunlight and saltwash. Inhale the sea notes of this seaweed before you open the bag. Salt combines with a twist of bitter to make a punchy accompaniment to fish or baking.

SEAWEED FLAVOUR BOOST

With seaweed we have the opportunity to start again with a whole set of new tastes and textures. Using seaweed in cooking is really about trusting your instincts, namely your taste buds. Close your eyes and taste? It is a delicate balancing act of sweet, sour, salt, bitter, umami, so no one taste dominates.

I have been amazed at the subtlety and delicacy of many of the flavours that come through if you let them, such as the Dashi Stock, which is as light as a fine chicken or marrow stock and just as fortifying too. If stock made from bones gives you a deep nourishment, so too with seaweed broth, which tastes of minerals, essential salts and the finest hint of sea spray.

Keep on checking the seasoning of your seaweed dishes; you will be amazed how much flavour even a small bit of seaweed can add. Stick to the umami-rich foods in the store cupboard (see page 25) and you cannot go wrong. My cupboard has been full of umami foods for years without my even knowing it: tins of tuna, sardines, tomato paste, olives, dried mushrooms, soy sauce, and fresh ginger, garlic and Parmesan in the fridge. It is all about having ingredients around you that work with seaweed to build flavours slowly.

Seaweed's synergy with other flavours makes it easy to fit into a family repertoire, whether it is soups, stews, pizzas or simple egg dishes. The main thing is to mix it up. Use bacon fat or gravy from game to complement your seaweed flavours or add it in as a pickled, lightly sautéed or crumbled addition. It will all add to the wonderful tastes that you create.

THE CANCER-PROTECTIVE ACTIONS OF SEAWEED

For many decades researchers in the field of cancer have been fascinated by the fact that the Japanese have very low rates of certain cancers, and it may be that aspects of their diet are the answer. The Japanese consume more seaweed than any other nation, therefore the possible link between this and cancer prevention has been the subject of numerous studies. Unfortunately the majority of this research has taken place in the lab or on animals and human studies are not yet available. However, ancient medicine practices such as Traditional Chinese and Ayurvedic have long used seaweed in their cancer treatments.

Not only is seaweed a rich source of many vitamins and minerals, which are known to be cancer protective, but also many types of brown seaweed contain a sulphur-rich polysaccharide called 'fucoidan'. There has been some research to show that this compound appears to inhibit cancer cell proliferation and induce the mechanism of apoptosis, or programmed cell death, in cancer cells. Fucoidan has also been found to be anti-inflammatory, antiviral and supportive of the immune system, all of which are of great importance in the reduction of cancer risk.

As our soils become depleted in certain minerals, land-grown foods may be deficient in crucial minerals. Zinc and selenium are important anti-cancer minerals and levels of these have been found to be significantly higher in seaweed, but it is the level of iodine it contains that may be of greatest significance where cancer is concerned. As soil levels of iodine drop, iodine deficiency amongst populations is becoming widely reported. Iodine is key to healthy thyroid function and thyroid hormones are key to the regulation of our metabolism, in other words the chemical transformations that take place within our cells. There is increasing research linking dysfunctional metabolism to increased cancer cell growth.

Tissues of the breast and prostate appear to have a high affinity to iodine and studies have linked a deficiency in this mineral to an increased risk of these particular cancers. Certain physical and biochemical properties of seaweed have also been shown to have a regulatory role in the production of oestrogen within the body, which may be behind seaweed's potential to protect against hormone-sensitive cancers.

The other properties of seaweed are its high antioxidant activity and its ability to bind to potentially carcinogenic toxins within the gut and eliminate them from the body. It also exhibits anti-angiogenesis properties, which mean it inhibits the formation of a vascular network to feed cancer cells and increase growth.

In the light of this knowledge so far, it would appear that incorporating seaweed into a plant rich, balanced diet may well be a very useful addition in our armoury against cancer.

Catherine Zabilowicz, author of *The Living Well with Cancer Cookbook* and nutrition advisor for Maggie's Cancer Centre, West London

THE CANCER-PROTECTIVE ACTIONS OF SEAWEED

SEAWEED AND ATHLETIC PERFORMANCE

The organic nature of seaweed is such that when it is ingested it can be broken down easily and our bodies can utilise the nutrients contained within it in order to function optimally.

It has the unique capacity to fill the nutrient gaps in our modern diets as it contains high levels of micronutrients (magic wands), which we need for everyday physiological and psychological function. These magic wands enable the body to produce enzymes, hormones and other substances essential for proper growth and development.

When we exercise our bodies, our need for micronutrients increases due to increased stress on the body and loss of salts through sweat.

Calcium
Skeletal health, heart health, nervous system function

Magnesium
Activates enzymatic activity, essential for heart health

Potassium
Naturally prevents high blood pressure, provides cellular energy

Sodium
Essential for the correct balance of body fluids

Iron
As haemoglobin transports and distributes oxygen to all your cells

Iodine
Thyroid health – production of thyroid hormones needed to increase cellular reaction including oxygen consumption and base metabolic rate

Chromium
Works with insulin to regulate blood sugar

Copper

Protects nerve sheaths, builds supply arteries required for iron absorption, absorbs and naturally reduces and eliminates radioactive elements and heavy metal contaminants from our bodies.

Louisa Copping, 2014

SEAWEED AND NUTRIENTS

Small changes to our diet can have a profound impact on our health. We all make numerous food choices every day and in my capacity as a nutritional therapist I've witnessed how clients have managed to improve their health by making informed decisions when it comes to food by including foods that heal and nourish.

Seaweed has been a food that I have always been aware of as having health benefits, although I knew it mainly from eating miso soup and sushi. Britain and Ireland have long traditions of using seaweed in their diets. A saying in pre-famine Ireland sums this up nicely in the considered order of care for the woman in the house, stating 'Potato, Children, Seaweed,' so the importance of seaweed was once ranked very high!

Since learning more about this amazing nutritional source I have been recommending it to people and using it myself in my own kitchen. I add seaweeds to family meals almost in the same way that I would use a spice and I find that it adds a lovely depth of flavour to dishes. Small amounts are enough to get a nutrient boost if eaten frequently. Seaweeds are so easy and versatile to use and they can be incorporated into salads, sprinkled onto eggs or thrown into smoothies, soups, pasta sauces or casseroles.

Seaweed is such a nutrient-dense food and eaten in food form the nutrients are put into our body in a bio-available way so, as a nutritional therapist and mum, it is very satisfying to see my family eating something I know is providing them with numerous health benefits.

There are many different types of seaweeds with varying nutritional properties. However, seaweeds in general all contain a broad range of nutrients such as iodine, calcium, potassium, zinc, iron, manganese, chromium and vitamins A, B, C and E. The abundance of antioxidants in seaweeds can help prevent cell damage in our body and improve the quality of our health by strengthening our immune system to be able to fight off the risk of infection.

The mineral-rich nature of seaweeds rests on the fact that, unlike land vegetables, which are limited to what nutrients they obtain from the increasingly poor soil, seaweeds are able to soak up the vast amount of minerals from what they bath in – the mineral-rich sea.

This high mineral content of seaweeds makes them a very alkalizing food as they are good sources of the alkalizing minerals calcium, potassium and magnesium. Eating alkalizing foods such as fruit, land vegetables and sea vegetables in our daily diet is important to maintain a healthy acid/alkaline balance in our bodies, but actually most people in the West eat a diet that is predominantly acidic owing to the high intake of meat, dairy and sugar. Over time this can start to take effect on the body as it works ever harder to maintain its acid/alkaline balance and the digestive system, liver and kidneys can come under strain. Inflammatory conditions, allergies, eczema, weight problems and digestive issues, including constipation and bloating, can all become potential problems with a highly acidic diet, so it's important that we eat a healthy balance and include alkalizing foods like seaweeds to counterbalance some of the more acidic foods in our diets.

Seaweed is fantastic for vegans, vegetarians and anyone wanting to reduce their meat or dairy intake as it has good levels of protein, calcium, iron and iodine. Dulse and Alaria have also got good levels of the vitamin B12, which is essential for nerve health and many cognitive functions, including memory, but which is usually only found in meat products. The health benefits behind lowering your meat intake include reducing the strain on your digestive system and reducing your saturated fat intake, which is good for your waistline and also your cardiovascular health. The Meatless Monday campaign was brought over to the UK with the aim of trying to challenge us to look beyond meat and to try a vegetarian option for just one day a week – even this small reduction in our meat consumption could have a positive impact on our health.

SEAWEED AND OUR HORMONES

Hormones are our body's master regulators as they are important chemical messengers that travel to other parts of our body where they help control how cells and organs work, regulating heart rate, metabolism and digestion. Our hormonal system could be supported by the inclusion of seaweed as it contains many of the nutrients the system needs to stay healthy, such as zinc, magnesium, and vitamins C and E.

Premenstrual symptoms can be an ongoing monthly battle for many women and can consist of breast tenderness, bloating, headaches and irritability. The inclusion of mineral- and vitamin-rich foods throughout the month can help to ease these symptoms and ensure that the body has sufficient nutrients to support its hormonal system. Seaweed is a good addition as it contains B6, zinc and magnesium, which can be beneficial in easing premenstrual symptoms.

Fertility could be supported by the inclusion of seaweed in our diets as it contains many of the key nutrients that our body needs to balance our hormones and support reproductive health, including vitamins B6, B12, C and E. In Korea, seaweed is also recommended for pregnant women and in the first 3 weeks after childbirth women are given seaweed soup three times a day as, according to the elders and Korean folklore, it is supposed to replenish and rejuvenate the body as well as help produce breast milk.

Kombu is extremely rich in iodine, and while iodine may be better known for its effect on the thyroid gland it is actually crucial for hormone balance overall. Deficiencies in iodine could be a contributing factor to many disorders of the hormone system such as thyroid conditions, diabetes, prostate disorders, auto-immune disorders, fibrocystic breast disease and polycystic ovary syndrome.

SEAWEED AND OUR THYROID

Iodine helps to regulate the thyroid gland, which is important for our mood, weight, body temperature, energy and health of our skin, hair and nails. Signs of an overactive thyroid include weight loss, nervousness and a high body temperature, while someone with an underactive thyroid gland can display weight gain, severe tiredness, cold extremities, constipation and oedema.

It is feared that iodine insufficiency is increasing in the UK, particularly in women of childbearing age and pregnant women. This is thought to be because of increasingly iodine-depleted soil levels and a decreasing consumption of milk and seafood. Seawater is high in iodine, which makes seafood the principal dietary source of this mineral. The brown seaweeds, including Kombu and Wakame, are particularly rich in iodine and we should be eating these little and often in order to keep our iodine at a sufficient level. The RNI (Reference Nutrient Intake) of iodine in the UK is 150mcg a day so we can actually get enough iodine by adding ½ teaspoon dried seaweed to our daily diet.

According to the World Health Organisation, this level increases for pregnant women to 220mcg a day and 290mcg for breastfeeding women. A sufficient quantity of iodine for pregnant and breastfeeding women is essential for the brain development of the baby. A deficiency in iodine can lead to intellectual disability and hearing and speech defects, while even a mild to moderate deficiency can lead to lower intelligence in children. The World Health Organisation has cited iodine deficiency as the most preventable cause of intellectual disability. This certainly highlights the importance of iodine. However, it is a mineral that we can also get too much of, something we need to be aware of, especially if we are looking at supplementation. There are some variations on what is considered a safe limit to the amount of iodine in our diet – the European upper safety limit is 600mcg, while the World Health Organisation considers 1,100mcg to be the safe upper limit.

The Japanese eat as much as 100 times the UK's RDA on a daily basis owing to their seaweed-rich diets, but there is a difference in the iodine that is found in dietary sources like seaweed from that in supplements. The iodine found in dietary sources is in chelated form, which is slow releasing so it acts as a gentle dose to the thyroid gland. I would recommend that we consume small quantities of seaweed regularly as the best way to get sufficient iodine through our diet.

SEAWEED AND OUR WEIGHT

The thyroid gland is notorious for being blamed for weight gain, as some suspect that an underactive thyroid could be partly responsible for weight that is difficult to shift. Sufficient iodine in the diet will help the thyroid to work optimally and could prove beneficial to those who suspect that their thyroid is working under par. Seaweed can help with weight loss as it is, as a whole, a low GI food, which means that it releases energy from food more slowly, which helps prevent large sugar highs and then the subsequent lows, which over time can lead to sugar cravings and eventually type 2 diabetes.

Seaweed is a naturally low-calorie and low-fat food that you are unlikely to binge on with its strong, smoky flavour. It also marries best with other healthy, healing foods – sushi, tofu, green salads and earthy vegetables, so this all makes seaweed a good nutritional food to include if you are looking for weight loss or to maintain your weight.

Seaweeds are packed with soluble fibre that slows down our digestive system and gives us the feeling of satiety, which can be beneficial for weight loss as it makes us feel fuller for longer. The University of Newcastle has proposed that a compound in seaweed could stop the body absorbing fat, which may prove beneficial in the fight against obesity. Initial findings have shown that seaweed fibres called alginates, which are found in Kombu, could suppress the digestion of fat in the gut. One variant of alginate compound curtailed fat absorption by up to 75% in initial experiments. Full clinical trials to test this proposal are being undertaken.

Soluble fibre is also hugely beneficial to our digestive health. Soluble fibre attracts water and turns into a gel in our body, which slows the absorption of cholesterol, which keeps our heart happy, and also the absorption of sugars, which helps to balance our blood sugar levels. Soluble fibre prevents constipation, which means that toxic waste that our body needs to clear is removed more quickly.

The polysaccharides in seaweeds also aid our digestive system as they exert a probiotic effect on the gut, which helps to regulate the normal functioning of the beneficial good bacteria and protects against the overgrowth of harmful bacteria.

Seaweed in itself is a great detoxifier and has long been used externally on the body in spas for this reason. When we consume seaweed, however, it also acts as an internal detoxifier and will mop up harmful chemicals from the body such as cadmium and lead, which are present in cigarette smoke and in heavily congested city air.

It only takes a small amount of seaweed in our diet to get a nutrient boost, so little and often is the key to using seaweed for the numerous potential health benefits that it can offer. This book has been written to teach us about the different types of seaweeds that are in plentiful supply and where we can source them. It also shows us, in a real and practical way, just how versatile and easy seaweed is to incorporate into our cooking and how to pair it with foods that work well with it and taste great.

Kerry Rae, DipION.

DIPS, SPREADS, RELISHES AND STOCKS

Eating well is about forward thinking; that way the hard work is done for you. It is about using what you already have in your larder as a starting point, and shaking in a bit of seaweed to transform your food. This section includes recipes as well as ideas for seasoning and flavouring dishes with marinades, relishes, pastes, dips and rubs made from special umami-rich seaweed preparations. Using a range of different spices, herbs and ingredients from land and sea, it is all about creating flavour.

BEAN AND DULSE DIP 🐝

This recipe is adapted from a Real Foods recipe. In the sixties my mum used to buy muesli and wholemeal products from there. It was the first organic shop in Edinburgh and is still going strong. This is a good solution if you have hungry people in the house who can't wait until dinner is ready. From start to finish it takes 10 minutes and can be lavishly spread onto flatbread or scooped up with chunky carrots. The Dulse gives it an even stronger umami factor.

SERVES 4–6

1 x 400g tin of cannellini beans
1 x 400g tin of red kidney beans
1 x 400g tin of flageolet beans
1 tablespoon Dulse flakes
4 tablespoons sun-dried tomato paste
2 teaspoons tamari or soy sauce

juice of 1 lime
salt and freshly ground black pepper
4 tablespoons Vegetable Stock (see page 51) or water
fresh basil leaves, to decorate

METHOD

➤ Drain the water from the tins of beans, put all the ingredients except the stock and basil leaves into a food processor and blend well. Keep adding stock or water until you get the consistency of a smooth paste.
➤ Chill in the fridge and decorate with basil leaves.
➤ Eat with crunchy vegetables or flatbread.

BEETROOT SEAWEED HUMMUS DIP 🌿

I love a table with jewel-coloured dips on it. You eat with your eyes as well as your stomach, remember. This will not disappoint and looks stunning spooned onto baby gem lettuce leaves. This is a root vegetable put with Kombu, which has a delicious earthy taste also. Finish off with seaweed sprinkle – perfection.

SERVES 4–6

1 tablespoon Kombu flakes
250g cooked beetroot, peeled
1 x 400g tin of chickpeas, drained
juice of 1 lemon
2 tablespoons tahini
2 teaspoons ground cumin
100ml rapeseed oil

a small bunch of fresh parsley,
  chopped
1 clove of garlic, crushed
1 tablespoon creamed horseradish
1 teaspoon Seaweed Sprinkle
  (see page 67)

METHOD

➤ Put all the ingredients in a food processor apart from the horseradish and seaweed sprinkle and pulse for a minute. Add a little more oil if not smooth enough.

➤ Using a spatula scoop out the mixture into a serving bowl, stir horseradish through it and finish off with Seaweed Sprinkle.

MACKEREL PÂTÉ WITH DULSE

One of my enduring favourites is mackerel pâté with anchovies. For those of you who use anchovies as a secret weapon to boost flavour and deepen the taste, I have a new proposition – Dulse. I have substituted it for anchovies because seaweed is local and plentiful, is less salty and does the same thing. Try in a green wrap of crunchy cos lettuce or in dollops on a chicory leaf.

SERVES 2–4

400g tinned mackerel in oil
juice and zest of 3 lemons
200g soft cheese
1 tablespoon Dulse flakes
a pinch of nutmeg
1 tablespoon finely chopped fresh flat-leaf parsley

METHOD

➤ Put all the ingredients into a food processor and blitz.
➤ Eat on flatbread or scoop up with celery or carrot sticks.

SANDWICH SPREAD IS BACK 🦋

This iconic spread is crying out to be updated. With the addition of seaweed it has got good, honest food written all over it. In terms of flavour and texture, it goes so well with gherkins, pickles and chunks of veg.

There was some debate about how big the chunks of carrot should be . . . we decided 1cm cubes make more of a statement. My family are happily taking this off for lunch spread in rolls and layered up with ham, cheese or lettuce. A nod to the seventies and how far we've come.

SERVES 4–6

5g whole leaf Sea lettuce or Kombu (1g if dried, rehydrated for 5 minutes in warm water)

1 small red onion, halved

50g cabbage (kale will do), roughly chopped

1 stick of celery, roughly chopped

1 teaspoon Dijon mustard

1 teaspoon mustard seeds

2 medium gherkins

1 tablespoon oil

1 teaspoon red wine vinegar

150g carrots, peeled, sliced lengthways and chopped into 1cm cubes

150g red peppers, deseeded, sliced lengthways and chopped into 1cm cubes

7 tablespoons Mayonnaise (see page 70 and add 1 teaspoon smoked Dulse for extra smoulder)

juice of ½ a lemon

freshly ground black pepper

sprig of fresh dill, chopped

METHOD

➤ Put the seaweed, onion, cabbage and celery in a food processor with the mustard, mustard seeds, gherkins, oil and vinegar for 20 to 30 seconds and blitz, but not too fine. Remove and scrape into a medium mixing bowl.

➤ Add in the diced carrot and pepper. Stir in the mayonnaise and mix thoroughly. Add the lemon juice and check the seasoning. Add some black pepper and fresh dill.

➤ Keep in the fridge – it won't last long, I guarantee.

KOMBU, MUSHROOM AND TARRAGON PÂTÉ 🌿

This pâté is up there with its meat brothers, like chicken liver and smoked salmon. Although vegetarian-friendly, it does not lack punch. The umami flavours of mushrooms, onions, garlic, miso and Kombu result in a complex and deeply delicious savoury spread. Don't be surprised if it gets scooped up with oatcakes or flatbread as it cools down and waits to go into the fridge.

SERVES 2–4

3–4 tablespoons good-quality rapeseed oil
1 red onion, finely chopped
3–4 cloves of garlic, crushed
250g chestnut mushrooms, thinly sliced
1 small glass of red wine

½ tablespoon Kombu flakes
½ tablespoon brown rice miso paste
a pinch of sea salt
a sprig of fresh tarragon, leaves picked off and chopped
warm flatbread, to serve

METHOD

➤ Heat the oil in a heavy-based saucepan and add the onion and garlic. Cook over a medium heat until the onion becomes translucent. Do not burn the garlic! Add in the mushrooms and cook for about 5 minutes until they soften.

➤ Throw in the wine, making sure that the heat is turned up until much of the liquid is absorbed. Finally, add the Kombu and mix around. Take off the heat.

➤ Tip the contents of the pan into the food processor and add the miso paste. Blitz for about 30 seconds and scoop into a bowl. Check the seasoning and add a pinch of sea salt if necessary. Add in the chopped tarragon and serve with warm flatbread.

DIPS, SPREADS, RELISHES AND STOCKS

47

CARROT AND GINGER RELISH 🌿

There are so many things that this Japanese fusion relish goes with and you can spice up ordinary dishes with this extraordinarily tasty concoction. It is good with plump white fish, cured fish, cold meats or even just eaten straight out of the jar. This is something I would have in my fridge all year round. Seaweed is often eaten in Japan and China in this sweet form.

4 large or 5 medium carrots
½ a red onion
4cm piece of fresh ginger
10cm strip of Kombu (rehydrated for
    5 minutes in warm water, or fresh)
2 tablespoons water
1 tablespoon mirin
1 tablespoon rapeseed oil
2 tablespoons soy sauce
salt and freshly ground black pepper

METHOD
➤ Put all the ingredients in a food processor except for the soy sauce and seasoning and blitz. If the consistency is still too dry, add another spoonful of water. Check the seasoning and add soy sauce to taste.

DASHI STOCK 🍂

This is a variation on one of the many ways to make dashi. This recipe was given to me by our harvester, Rory MacPhee, who knows an awful lot about flavour and life generally. Dashi is a clean, delicate taste and well worth taking the trouble over. It doesn't take long and makes your miso soup taste extra delicious. All you need is a packet of dried Kombu tucked away in your cupboard.

This will also give you an injection of iodine to help get your digestion and energy levels back on track.

MAKES 1 LITRE OF STOCK

1 litre of water

1 11g blade of dried or fresh Kombu (2 strips of 15cm)

10g dried Dulse (rehydrated for 5 minutes in warm water),
  thinly sliced (optional)

1 thumb-size piece of fresh ginger

50g dried mushrooms (any will do, shitake are the strongest)

METHOD

➤ Measure out the water and put in a pan with the strips of Kombu. Soak for a few hours.

➤ Bring the pan of water almost to the boil. Just before it is about to bubble up, remove the Kombu and put aside.

➤ When you remove the Kombu from the soup, cut it up into tiny matchstick-size pieces. Add a tablespoon of water and a thumb-size piece of peeled, chopped fresh ginger. Eat immediately! This is almost my favourite way of eating seaweed.

➤ Simmer the stock with the dried mushrooms. After 20 minutes, put the thin slices of Dulse in (if using). Allow to cool and keep in the fridge for up to a week, or freeze until needed.

NOTE

Free MSG precipitates together with salt and mannitol to form a white layer on the surface of the dried and aged Kombu blade. This layer should not be removed before the dashi is extracted from the Kombu.

Dried whole leaf Alaria (*page 27*).

Beetroot seaweed hummus dip (*page 44*) with
Mooie's flatbread (*page 124*).

Seaweed butters: Sea lettuce butter (top right); Dulse butter with chilli and lime (top left); smoked Dulse butter (middle left); Dulse and radish butter (bottom right); Shony lemon chilli butter (*pages 59–60*).

Kale and Sea lettuce pesto with walnuts (*page 74*).

Seaweed salts: Nori and chilli salt (top right); Kombu, fennel and lemon salt (top left); rose and Dulse; quail's egg salt (bottom left); smoked Dulse and cloves (bottom right) (*page 65*).

Sunshine smoothie (*page 85*).

Nurturing almond milk with Carragheen and chocolate (*page 86*).

Chilled Alaria soup (*page 93*).

VEGETABLE STOCK 🌿

This is a building block stock, with the boost of a piece of seaweed put into the brew to give added minerals. To this base you could add simple noodles, strips of vegetable or even some rice to make a good, nourishing, soupy dish.

MAKES APPROXIMATELY 1 LITRE

2 tablespoons rapeseed oil

2 large carrots, roughly chopped

2 sticks of celery, chopped into quarters

2 large onions, roughly chopped

350g mushrooms, sliced

1 medium potato, chopped

1 finger-size piece of fresh ginger, peeled and sliced

4 spring onions

a small bunch of fresh parsley

piece of dried Kombu leaf

2 litres water

METHOD

➤ Put the oil in a large heavy-based saucepan on a medium heat. Add the carrot, celery and onion. Cook for 10 minutes until softened. Add the mushrooms and stir for about 5 minutes until they have absorbed some of the juices. Keep the heat down, so that the vegetables cook slowly.

➤ Add the potato, ginger, spring onions, parsley, Kombu and the water. Bring to the boil, cover and simmer for about 1 hour.

➤ Sieve the stock and allow to cool, then keep covered in the fridge.

TIP

If you put dashi in with vegetables in a stock, you draw out the flavour of the vegetables.

DIPS, SPREADS, RELISHES AND STOCKS

SHONY HARISSA 🐟

When Fiona and I first started Mara in the early days of market-testing, we took a whole lot of dried ground seaweed samples into Moro for chef Sam Clark to try. He exchanged our samples for a dab of harissa, preserved lemons and a bag of sumac. We were delighted as these were ingredients that were hard to come by then. They go so well together that this Shony harissa was an obvious combining of flavours.

SERVES 6

8 red peppers

2 red chillies

2 tablespoons of good-quality rapeseed oil

2 teaspoons black poppy seeds

1 tablespoon coriander seeds

1 teaspoon caraway seeds

1 tablespoon cumin seeds

2 teaspoons freshly ground black pepper

1 tablespoon fennel seeds

2 tablespoons Shony flakes

good quality olive oil

1 clove of garlic, grated

zest of 9 lemons

1 teaspoon chilli flakes

salt and freshly ground black pepper

METHOD

➤ Preheat the oven to 200°C/Gas 6. Roast the red peppers and the chillies drizzled with rapeseed oil until parts start to blacken and they are completely soft.

➤ Grind the black poppy seeds, coriander seeds, caraway, cumin, black pepper, fennel seeds, Shony and a little olive oil in a pestle and mortar until it reaches a paste. You may have to do this in batches, depending on the size of your pestle and mortar.

➤ Deseed your red peppers but keep your chillies whole, then mix in a food processor with your grated garlic clove to a chunky paste (according to how chunky you like your harissa).

➤ Slowly add to your pestle and mortar mixture along with the oil. Again, you may have to do this in batches.

➤ Mix in your lemon zest and chilli flakes, and season to taste. If you leave your harissa overnight it will become more spicy as the flavours mature.

UMAMI PASTE 🍌

This is a Nobu-inspired recipe, which works on the basis that complementary umami-rich foods work well together. Here we have leftover scraps of everyday veg, which are likely to be in most people's kitchens and usually end up in the compost. Not only are these bits of the vegetable (stalks, not leaves) the most nutritious, along with the skins, but they are full of flavour. If you have any pieces of seaweed that won't make the grade, throw them in too.

500g vegetable peelings and scraps from the following:
tomato seeds (they have more umami flavour than other bits of the tomato)
broccoli stems
green part of the spring onions/leeks
carrot, celeriac or parsnip peel
1 chilli pepper
1 clove of garlic
3 pieces of dried Kombu leaf
½ a jalapeno pepper

METHOD
➤ Combine all the above in a food processor and blitz. Stick in the fridge in a sealed container to let the flavours infuse. This should last for up to a week. Delicious pasted onto fish.

NOTE
Kombu contains large amounts of free amino acids of which 80 to 90% are glutamic acid in the form of MSG. This is what gives the umami hit.

DIPS, SPREADS, RELISHES AND STOCKS

SEAWEED ESSENCE

This sauce renders soy sauce and nam pla a bit redundant. It has sweetness and it has almost a truffly depth to it, where the umami flavour of the seaweed has become rich and complex. This is quick to make and is a brew that could add serious flavour to all your soups, stews, relishes and dips. Leave it bottled in an airtight container in a cool, dark place and you have a taste that will keep on deepening in flavour.

MAKES 200ML

4 tablespoons Dulse flakes

500ml warm water, to cover

½ teaspoon allspice

2 cloves, crushed

1 teaspoon sugar

2 teaspoons white wine vinegar

½ teaspoon agar agar powder (optional – to add viscosity)

½ teaspoon tomato purée

METHOD

➤ Put the Dulse in a pan and cover with the warm water. Bring nearly to the boil until bubbles start rising to the surface, then take off the heat and leave with a lid over it for 20 minutes.

➤ When cool, sieve and pour into a jar, then add the allspice, cloves, sugar, vinegar and agar agar powder (this will make it more viscous) and tomato purée.

➤ This will keep for at least 2 to 3 weeks in the fridge if the jar is firmly sealed.

NOTE

The umami hit you get from this sauce may well be due to the fact that Dulse is high in protein. It boasts the highest content of iron of any food source. It also contains all the essential amino acids, iodine, calcium, phosphorus, potassium and magnesium, manganese and vitamins A, C, D and B complex.

SEAWEED BUTTERS

Incorporating the flavours of the different seaweeds into butters is a no brainer; they look stunning and are easy to use. Sweet and savoury, there is hardly a mealtime when you would be without a seaweed fillip. It is best to use good-quality butter since the end result will be creamier and smoother. Flakes and powders work well with butters since the finer the seaweed, the bigger the taste. Add more seaweed for a stronger infused butter. It's a question of taste.

DULSE AND RADISH BUTTER 🌿

4–6 PORTIONS
100g red radishes
3 tablespoons unsalted butter (softened dairy-free butter can be used)
1 tablespoon Dulse flakes
a pinch of sea salt
a pinch of white pepper

METHOD
➤ Put the radishes in a food processor and blitz for a few seconds. Remove from the mixer and lay on paper towels to remove excess moisture.
➤ Transfer to a medium bowl and add 2 tablespoons of the butter and the Dulse. Using a spatula add the rest of the butter, stirring the mixture until the radish and Dulse are incorporated thoroughly.
➤ Transfer to ramekins or small bowls and cover in cling film. Chill until required, then remove the cling film and scatter with a little sea salt and pepper.
➤ Eat with crunchy salad leaves, celery or on crackers.

ALMOND AND DULSE BUTTER 🌿

Although this sounds counterintuitive, there is no butter in this. It takes no time at all to turn a bag of nuts and a spoonful or two of seaweed into a glorious, swirling butter. If you are a peanut or cashew person, you can substitute the appropriate nuts. Eat with celery sticks or sprinkle with grated carrot and dollop onto an oatcake.

300g unsalted almonds
2 tablespoons Dulse flakes
3 tablespoons good-quality olive oil

METHOD
➤ Put the almonds in a food processor with the Dulse and mix until it forms first a flour and then a butter. This may take a few minutes. Add

the oil until it reaches the right consistency. Scrape the creamy nut butter out of the bowl with a spatula into a jar or container and keep in the fridge. It will keep for a couple of weeks.

All the following butters can be kept in the freezer and slices taken off them to melt over white fish or seafood. They will keep for up to 5 days in the fridge.

DULSE/SMOKED DULSE BUTTER 🌿

50g unsalted butter
1 teaspoon Dulse flakes/smoked Dulse powder
a generous pinch of sea salt

DULSE BUTTER WITH CHILLI AND LIME 🌿

50g unsalted butter
1 teaspoon Dulse flakes
a pinch of dried chilli flakes (ground finely)
juice of ½ lime
a generous pinch of sea salt

SHONY, LEMON AND CHILLI BUTTER 🌿

50g unsalted butter
1 teaspoon Shony flakes
a pinch of chilli flakes
1 teaspoon lemon juice
a generous pinch of sea salt

SEA LETTUCE BUTTER 🦋

50g unsalted butter
1 teaspoon Sea lettuce flakes
a generous pinch of sea salt

METHOD
➤ Take a pack of butter out of the fridge and allow it to become medium
  soft – this may take a few hours. Put the butter in a food processor
  until it is smooth and creamy, but do not allow it to become too soft.
  Add the seaweed flakes and sea salt in a steady stream to make sure
  they are evenly distributed. Add the other ingredients and mix well.
  Scrape out of the bowl with a spatula onto a piece of cling film about
  15cm square on a flat dinner plate.
➤ Fold the cling film over the butter and roll until you get a sausage
  shape. Undo the cling film and move the butter near the edge of it. Roll
  the edge neatly over the butter and roll again so that you have no
  wrinkles. Fold in the ends like an envelope and put into the fridge to
  harden – this will take a few hours.

The butters can be frozen and slices cut off them as and when they are
required.

TIP
To make scrambled egg and Dulse butter, spread your toast with Dulse
butter and top with creamy scrambled eggs made with a dollop of cream.
An old savoury, refashioned. Seriously good.

SEAWEED SALTS, RUBS AND SAUCES

Middle-Eastern herbs like sumac or za'atar blend well with seaweed's sweet-salt notes, while equally you can move towards Asian spices such as cardamom, cinnamon and cumin or lean more to the Mediterranean, with aromatic herbs like rosemary, thyme and oregano. I have included a pinch of sea salt to add more intensity to the flavours. Not only do the salts look beautiful but you have created a little piece of stardust. A little goes a long way.

ROSE AND DULSE SALT ✤

(for beef, lamb, game, chocolate)
½ teaspoon sea salt
a pinch of rose petals
1 tablespoon Dulse flakes
¼ fresh red chilli, finely chopped
¼ teaspoon pink peppercorns

NORI AND CHILLI SALT ✤

(for pork, duck, chicken, fish, seafood)
½ teaspoon sea salt
1 tablespoon roasted Nori flakes
½ teaspoon chilli flakes
½ teaspoon sumac

KOMBU, FENNEL AND LEMON SALT ✤

(for fish, pork, chicken, savoury baking, chocolate)
½ teaspoon sea salt
1 tablespoon Kombu flakes
½ teaspoon fennel seeds
zest of ½ lemon
4 cardamom seeds

SMOKED DULSE AND CLOVES SALT ✤

(works on barbecued meat, pizzas, goulashes, stews)
½ teaspoon sea salt
1 tablespoon smoked Dulse flakes
¼ teaspoon cayenne pepper
¼ teaspoon ground ginger

2 cloves

*For a BBQ rub add 1 tablespoon brown sugar

DRY-RUB METHOD

➤ Grind up all the spices and seaweed in a pestle and mortar, or in a heavy bowl with a rolling pin bash all the spices to release the flavour bomb.

NOTE

Cutting down salt usage by half would make a big difference to overall health. Reducing salt intake by 1g per day would prevent more than 6000 deaths from strokes and heart attacks per year and save the NHS £288m per annum.[15] Seaweed has less sodium than table or gourmet salt.

SEAWEED SPRINKLE 🐟

This is a seaweed sprinkle, which is traditionally used in Japan as a topping for rice and fish dishes or eaten as a snack or healthy salt alternative, and is known as furikake. Here I have not used bonito flakes or artificial MSG. The amounts can be adjusted if you don't like chilli or if you would prefer a pinch of sugar to sweeten, as they do in Japan.

25g white sesame seeds
25g black sesame seeds
1 tablespoon roasted Nori flakes (you can also
    crumble a sheet into small pieces)
2 tablespoons Dulse flakes
¼ teaspoon smoked paprika
a small pinch of chilli flakes
a small pinch of celery salt

METHOD
➤ Toast the sesame seeds in a flat-bottomed frying pan on a high heat
    until the white seeds become golden and start popping. Be careful not
    to burn them. Take off the heat and put into a small bowl.
➤ Add in the Nori, Dulse, paprika, chilli and celery salt.
➤ Keep in a moisture-free container in a cool place.

TIP
If your Nori is not roasted, you can toast it in the oven for 2 to
3 minutes.

SEAWEED SALTS, RUBS AND SAUCES

CHICKEN SEASONING

Chicken and Kombu are both umami foods. Put them together and you have a savoury fusion of deliciousness.

SERVES 4

1 whole chicken (free range)
2 spring onions, finely chopped
1 clove of garlic, crushed (or wild garlic if in season)
2 teaspoons Kombu flakes
½ teaspoon paprika
1 teaspoon demerara sugar or honey
1 tablespoon rapeseed oil

METHOD

➤ Add the spring onions and garlic to the dry ingredients, then add the oil.
➤ Smear all over the chicken, make incisions in the chicken skin with a sharp knife and push the rub under it, making sure the wonderful flavours are well rubbed in.
➤ Roast the chicken as usual.

THYME, CINNAMON AND DULSE RUB FOR LAMB

This is a good alternative to the classic rosemary option. The thyme works really well with the anchovy-like Dulse flavours that melt into the lamb as it roasts, while the cinnamon adds sweetness, which complements the saltiness of the seaweed.

SERVES 6–8

1 leg of lamb
a large bunch of fresh thyme
1 teaspoon ground cinnamon
1 large tablespoon Dulse flakes
2 tablespoons rapeseed oil
5 cloves of garlic, halved lengthwise
a pinch of sea salt

METHOD

➤ Strip the thyme leaves off their stalks and release their flavour by crushing in a pestle and mortar with the cinnamon and Dulse.
➤ Cover the outside of the leg of lamb or rub on the inside of a butterfly with the dry rub. Drizzle over the oil and make sure all the aromatic flavours are well rubbed into the skin and the meat. Stud the meat with the garlic cloves using the tip of a sharp knife and sprinkle on the sea salt.
➤ Cook the lamb according to its weight in a 200°C/Gas 6 oven.

MAYONNAISE/AIOLI 🌿

This is a recipe that can be tailored to whatever you are eating. For a straightforward mayonnaise, cut out most of the garlic; add smoked Dulse and a pinch of cayenne pepper for dressed crab mayonnaise. If it is prawn cocktail, add tomato purée and smoked Dulse. Add wasabi for some heat and citrus for lemon mayonnaise; garden herbs in your mayonnaise could take it in another direction.

1 egg
3 egg yolks
1 clove of garlic, crushed
3 teaspoons Dulse flakes or powder or smoked Dulse
    (for dressed crab or prawn cocktail)
125ml light olive oil
125ml good-quality olive oil
salt and freshly ground pepper

VARIATIONS:
a pinch of cayenne pepper (for dressed crab or prawn cocktail)
1 teaspoon tomato purée (for prawn cocktail)
½ garlic bulb, cloves peeled and separated (for aioli)
½ teaspoon wasabi paste (for wasabi mayonnaise)
a squeeze of lemon juice (for lemon mayonnaise)
1 tablespoon fresh parsley, coriander, basil, chopped (for herb
    mayonnaise)

METHOD
➤ Put the egg, egg yolks, garlic and Dulse (or smoked Dulse for dressed crab or prawn cocktail) in a food processor and blend.
➤ Add the oils in a thin, steady stream while the machine is going.
➤ Finally, add the cayenne pepper, tomato purée, garlic cloves, wasabi, lemon juice or herbs, if using, and seasoning to taste.

SMOKED DULSE HOLLANDAISE ✿

SERVES 2–4

200g unsalted butter
2 free-range egg yolks
½ tablespoon lemon juice
1 teaspoon smoked Dulse flakes or powder
a pinch of cayenne pepper
salt and freshly ground black pepper

METHOD

➤ Melt the butter on a medium hot ring. Do not let it boil.
➤ Put the egg yolks, lemon juice, smoked Dulse and cayenne in a food
  processor or blender and blitz for a minute or so.
➤ Add the melted butter in a thin stream with the blender constantly
  on – you are aiming for a thick, creamy custard-like consistency. If it is
  too thick add some warm water.
➤ Check for seasoning. Add more lemon juice or another pinch of
  smoked Dulse if too bland. Keep warm until you assemble your dish.

SEAWEED SALTS, RUBS AND SAUCES

WATERCRESS KOMBU PURÉE 🐟

There are times when you need a shot of optimism, a reminder that there are green shoots under the dead mulch of winter. For me, this bright green purée does it. Tastewise, not only do you get the subtle pepperiness of the watercress, but you get the salt definition of the Kombu. This is good with a piece of fresh salmon and some plain white rice.

SERVES 4–6

200g frozen peas
400g watercress, washed and long stalks removed
    (spinach can be substituted)
40g Kombu (3 x 15cm blades of dried Kombu,
    rehydrated for 5 minutes in warm water)
30g unsalted butter
a pinch of sea salt
a squeeze of lemon

METHOD

➤ Put a pan of water on the hob and bring to the boil. Add the peas,
   return to the boiling point and cook for 5 minutes.
➤ At this point turn off the heat and add the watercress and the Kombu.
   Put a lid on so that the watercress wilts into the peas. Leave for
   5 minutes and drain.
➤ Put into a food processor with the butter and blitz for a few minutes.
   Add the salt and squeeze of lemon and check the seasoning.

SEAWEED SALTS, RUBS AND SAUCES

KALE AND SEA LETTUCE PESTO WITH WALNUTS 🌿

This makes a change from the classic basil pesto. In the summer you could swap kale for spinach, and the fact it uses walnuts not pine nuts is good for the pine forests. There is some serious boosting here from the Sea lettuce. This could be eaten on pasta or rice, or spread on a piece of toast with some meat or cheese.

SERVES 4–6

1 whole bulb and 2 cloves of garlic
50g kale, leaves removed from stalks
2 tablespoons Sea lettuce flakes
juice of ½ lemon
60g walnuts or cashews, chopped
1 tablespoon rapeseed oil
60g grated Parmesan cheese

METHOD

➤ Heat the oven to 200°C/Gas 6. Cut the top off the head of the bulb of garlic and sprinkle with oil. Wrap in tin foil and place on a baking tray in the oven for 20 minutes until soft and sweet. When it is cool, squeeze into kale and Sea lettuce mixture with the garlic, lemon juice, walnuts and half of the oil and blitz in a food processor until well combined. Add the Parmesan and the rest of the oil and mix for a few seconds. Add some hot water if too thick.

➤ Serve as a relish or side dish with fish or vegetarian food.

NOTE

For vegetarians Sea lettuce is one of the few vegetable sources of B12.

BASIC PASTA SAUCE WITH TOMATO, OLIVES AND DULSE 🌿

There is something about the flavour combination of tomatoes, black olives and Dulse. They go together so well. This is a safe and good base for a quick pasta sauce. Make sure you include the tomato seeds and skins as this is where all the umami is concentrated.

SERVES 4–6

1 onion, finely chopped
2 tablespoons rapeseed oil
a knob of butter
2 cloves of garlic, finely chopped
100g mushrooms, cleaned and
    sliced
500g ripe tomatoes, roughly
    chopped

100g black pitted olives
1 tablespoon Dulse flakes
1 tablespoon soy sauce
a small bunch of fresh parsley,
    finely chopped
a pinch of salt (optional)

METHOD

➤ Sauté the onion in a heavy-based saucepan with the oil and butter for 5 minutes on a medium heat. Add in the garlic and stir until softened. Add the mushrooms and mix around until they are nearly cooked. Tip in the tomatoes and olives and simmer for 5 minutes or until the tomatoes are soft and fleshy.

➤ When cooked through, add the Dulse and soy sauce. Stir thoroughly and sprinkle on the parsley. Check the seasoning, adding a pinch of salt if necessary.

➤ Serve on top of buttered pasta or over rice.

NOTE
Seaweed contains potassium, which can lower blood pressure so is beneficial to cardiovascular health.

SALSA VERDE WITH ADDED UMAMI 🌿

This is a variation of Jamie Oliver's salsa verde, but with a few adjustments. I don't want to buy over-salted anchovies whose provenance is not always known when I can substitute them for home-grown Dulse. This has kick, and you can taste the umami notes of the Dulse coming through the fresh green herbs. This is a good stock item for the fridge, to have with cold meats or fish.

SERVES 4–6

2 cloves of garlic

1 tablespoon capers

1 tablespoon gherkins

2 large bunches of fresh parsley

a small handful of fresh basil

a small bunch of fresh mint leaves

1 tablespoon Dijon mustard

2 tablespoons red wine vinegar

1 tablespoon Dulse flakes

6 tablespoons good-quality rapeseed oil

freshly ground black pepper

METHOD

➤ Put all the ingredients into a food processor and blitz. Add more oil if it is not liquid enough. Keep in an airtight jar.

DRINKS AND JUICES

To me, seaweed means 'recovery' and 'tonic'. Infusing, liquidizing or stirring seaweed into drinks means that you can recharge your batteries and clear out your system on a deep level. Nourish, nurture, drink, replenish.

Adapt your ingredients according to the season: spring greens when winter is over, dark green kales when they come into season. You can't go wrong . . . that is if you remember to put the seaweed in.

This section contains recipes for people who are in a hurry, but want all the benefits of seaweed. A teaspoon in a smoothie will put the salts back in your body and give you your mojo back. There's also a cocktail for those slightly less wholesome moments.

CHANNEL WRACK, LEMON AND GINGER INFUSION ⚘

This infusion of Channel Wrack (or Pelvetia) has a delicate, citrus zing with a slight hint of salt. It would be a perfect tonic to take in a flask or sports bottle on a long walk, hike or bike ride. A tangy brew to restore your balance and replace the electrolytes.

SERVES 4

30g dried Channel Wrack (or a small handful)
    (rehydrated for 30 minutes in warm water)
1 litre boiling water
zest and juice of 1 lemon
2 thumb-size pieces of fresh ginger, peeled and sliced thinly
2 cardamom pods, opened
1 tablespoon honey (Manuka for added health benefits)

METHOD

➤ Squeeze the water out of the soaked seaweed.
➤ Boil a kettle and add the litre of boiled water to a tea pot with the seaweed in. Stir and leave to infuse overnight or for 6 hours.
➤ Turn the hob ring onto a medium heat and pour the infused seaweed tea through a fine sieve or muslin into a medium-sized saucepan. Heat the liquid up with the lemon, ginger and cardamom. Sieve again. Sweeten with honey to taste.
➤ For the perfect power drink, add coconut water or pomegranate juice to the brew, but double the seaweed amount in the pot.

NOTE

Channel Wrack (*Pelvetia canaliculata*) is harvested in the Hebrides as a global nutriceutical for its valuable minerals and vitamins. It is a near relation of Bladderwrack and has similar properties, providing a tonic for your digestion and giving your metabolism and general body an overall boost. It is also rich in antioxidants such as vitamin E, which benefits skin health and promotes hormone balance.

BLADDERWRACK TEA 🌿

Bladderwrack (*Fucus vesiculosus*) might be my desert island re-balancer (along with the Kelly Kettle and matches so I can turn it into an infusion with minimum fuss). Nutritionally, you could not want for much more.

Earl Grey adds some dry, smoky notes, combined with the delicate salt taste of the seaweed. The honey adds a final sweetener to give you energy.

SERVES 4

30g dried Bladderwrack (a small handful)
   (rehydrated for 30 minutes in warm water)
3 Earl Grey tea bags to 1 litre boiled water
   (green tea bags can be used, if desired)
1 teaspoon honey

METHOD

➤ Squeeze the water out of the soaked seaweed.
➤ Boil a kettle and add a litre of boiled water to a tea pot with 3 Earl Grey tea bags. Add in the seaweed and stir. Leave to infuse overnight or for 6 hours.
➤ Turn the hob ring onto a medium heat and pour the infused seaweed tea through a strainer into a medium-sized saucepan. Heat the liquid up and add a spoonful of honey, or to taste.
➤ This can be mixed with pomegranate or cranberry juice to make an iced tea. Keep cold in the fridge and put in a sports bottle for your home-made power drink. Drink and revive!

NOTE

Bladderwrack has anti-viral, anti-parasitic, fungal and bacterial properties. It also encourages mucous stimulation in our digestive tract – in short, it keeps our gut healthier and helps mineralize the body.

LEAN GREEN SEAWEED TONIC SMOOTHIE 🐝

Kellie Anderson, nutritionist, food blogger @food to glow, and supporter of Maggie's Centres, has made up a smoothie that is absolutely delicious and good for your overall health.

SERVES 2

150–200ml coconut water or water

¼ pineapple, skin removed but core kept (it is very nutritious), cut into chunks or wedges

½ cucumber, cut into chunks

1 lime, peeled

2 sticks of celery

2 handfuls of spinach or baby kale

10 fresh mint leaves, plus more to taste once you have made the juice

1 thumb-size piece of fresh peeled turmeric or ginger (both are highly anti-inflammatory and great for gut health)

1 teaspoon Kombu or Dulse flakes

1 teaspoon matcha (Japanese green tea) (optional)

METHOD

➢ Place all the ingredients in a juicer or powerful blender in the order listed. Blend until smooth and enjoy immediately.

NOTE

'Pineapple, ginger, seaweed and mint are great for digestion, with mint especially being known to help calm indigestion and symptoms of IBS. Pineapple helps to break down food protein in the stomach. All of the ingredients are high in various anti-inflammatory compounds so are great for overall health.'
   Kellie Anderson, MSc

ONE FOR THE WOMEN ✿

I asked Jamie Sawyer, a strength and conditioning coach who is currently helping a friend work out, what he suggested as the ultimate female boosting drink. This is what he came back with.

SERVES 2

400ml green tea

60g assorted greens – broccoli, spinach, kale (whatever you have to hand, but alternate if you can)

1 teaspoon ground cinnamon

1 unripe banana (sugar spike less pronounced)

a handful of fruit (pomegranate seeds, kiwi, frozen raspberries, pears, blueberries for sweetness)

1 tablespoon Kombu flakes

1 dried whole leaf Alaria (or Wakame) (rehydrated for 5 minutes in warm water), finely chopped

METHOD

➤ First boil the kettle to make your green tea. Allow to cool.

➤ Rinse, drain, then chop your assortment of greens. Peel and roughly chop your fruit.

➤ Put all your ingredients into your blender (a high powered/speed one is recommended with fibrous ingredients and nuts, etc.). Blitz. Drink. Feel fantastic!

NOTE

The greens here are good for heart, calcium and oestrogen removal, while green tea helps with fat burning and the fruit is also full of antioxidants. The seaweed is good for everything. Kombu and Alaria are both rich in iodine and Alaria is loaded with calcium and magnesium (good for guarding against osteoporosis) while its pigment, fucoxanthin, is known to burn fatty tissue.

SUNSHINE SMOOTHIE 🍌

My friend Jane told me about a luxury retreat she used to go to in Thailand to escape Christmas. This drink is in honour of all those people who can't get away, but deserve a pick-me-up. The seaweed in the smoothie gets us a bit closer to the lapping waves and the white sand.

SERVES 2

1 under ripe banana
350ml coconut water
1 teaspoon ground cinnamon
1 teaspoon vanilla pod seeds
(cut the pod lengthways and
scrape out with a teaspoon
handle)

1 teaspoon oatmeal
1 teaspoon matcha (Japanese
green tea) (optional)
1 teaspoon Dulse flakes
3 ice cubes

METHOD

➢ Blitz all the ingredients in a blender, pour into a long glass and breathe.

NOTE

Japanese women consume on average 6g of seaweed per day. Their intake of iodine is 25 times higher than the average US woman[16] and their incidence of breast cancer rates is roughly one third lower:[17, 18] could their average consumption of 6g per day of seaweed be the reason?

NURTURING ALMOND MILK WITH CARRAGHEEN AND CHOCOLATE 🐚

Maraman, or Rory, doses the harvesters and office workers with this in the cold winter months (thanks Rory for caring). Not only does it make us feel nurtured, but nourished. The brew becomes gloriously creamy as Carragheen is a natural thickener – you may even have to eat it with a spoon. The shaved chocolate on the top is a nice addition that sends your brain a direct message that good things are on the way.

SERVES 4

20g (a small handful) dried Carragheen

1 litre almond (coconut, would do) milk

½ thumb-size piece of fresh ginger

1 cinnamon stick

1 cardamom pod, opened up

½ star anise

1 teaspoon allspice

1 tablespoon honey (Manuka for added anti-viral health benefits)

a pinch of nutmeg

1 teaspoon shaved chocolate

METHOD

➤ Soften the Carragheen in a bowl of warm water for 10 minutes to loosen all the wonderful seaweed oils.

➤ In the meantime, put a pan of milk on a medium ring to heat up. Squeeze the water out of the Carragheen and place in the milk with the ginger, cinnamon stick, cardamom pod, star anise and allspice.

➤ Bring to the boil and simmer gently for about 20 minutes until all the ingredients have infused the milk. Strain through a sieve (or muslin) and let the brew do the work. Stir in the honey and top with nutmeg or chocolate. Or both.

NOTE

Carragheen is beneficial for our mucous membranes. Traditionally, it has been used to help coughs and colds because it acts as a tonic for our respiratory sytem.

VIRGIN BLOODY MARA 🦪

'Our drink consisted of pure water, to which the Captain added some drops of a fermented liquor, extracted by the Kamschatcha method from a seaweed known under the name of Rhodomenia palmata.'

20,000 *Leagues Under the Sea*, Jules Verne

Mara is Gaelic for 'of the sea', and the name of our company. This classic tomato drink needs to be spiced up with some seaweed. Fruits of the vine meeting fruits of the sea.

The seaweed here takes the place of a salty, briny extra like Clamato, which is my guilty pleasure – expensive and hard to find. This is liquid umami and should be drunk not just after a heavy night, but in celebration of the fact that veg from the sea can taste amazing too.

SERVES 4
1 litre tomato juice
juice of 2 lemons
2 teaspoons Seaweed Essence (see page 54) or Dulse flakes
a dash or two of Worcestershire sauce
1 teaspoon horseradish
a pinch of celery salt
1 stick of celery
1 tablespoon Kombu flakes

METHOD
➤ Stir all the ingredients together except the celery stick and Kombu flakes. Dip the celery stick into the Kombu and add to the glass.
➤ Add a measure of vodka per glass to give it a kick.

SOUPS AND SALADS

CUCUMBER AND TARRAGON SOUP WITH KOMBU

This recipe is one that my stepmother made for me a few years ago and at the time I thought how big and bold the flavour was, despite it having no stock in it. The aniseed notes of the tarragon really complement the earthy taste of the Kombu, which introduces a bit of salt into the dish. A dollop of natural yoghurt finishes it off perfectly. Whatever the weather, this is fresh and vibrant.

SERVES 4

1 large cucumber
a small bunch of fresh tarragon, leaves picked
2 teaspoons Kombu flakes
6 ice cubes
100ml cold water
a small pinch of sea salt
4 tablespoons natural yoghurt

METHOD

➤ Chop the cucumber into four (seeds and all) and put in a food processor with the tarragon, Kombu, ice cubes and water. Blitz for a few seconds until you have a smooth, even liquid.
➤ Pour into a bowl and check the seasoning. If necessary, add a pinch of sea salt.
➤ Serve with a dollop of natural yoghurt.

SOUPS AND SALADS

CELTIC KELPIE – CHICKEN SOUP WITH ALMOND, KALE AND DULSE

Described on the menu of the Union of Genius soup café in Edinburgh as 'a delicate but substantial chicken and Dulse broth', this will warm the cockles. Union of Genius don't just cook with seaweed, they buy local, deliver by bike and reward their customers for returning their take-out packaging. They also donate soup to rough sleepers every night of the year. Union of Genius is right on the button.

SERVES 4–6

1 large onion, finely chopped
4 cloves of garlic, crushed
1 leek, finely sliced
50g butter
a dash of oil
2 large potatoes, finely chopped
1.5 litres chicken stock

1 or 2 chicken legs
50g toasted almonds
freshly ground black pepper
2 heaped teaspoons Dulse flakes
1 teaspoon horseradish sauce
a dash of double cream
100g shredded kale

METHOD

➤ Sauté the onion, garlic and leek in the butter with a dash of oil.
➤ Add the potatoes and the stock. Bring to a boil, add the chicken legs and simmer for 40 minutes. Remove the chicken and allow to cool a little. Shred the meat and add back into the soup.
➤ Add the toasted almonds, pepper, Dulse, horseradish and cream. Allow to cool and sit for a few hours (ideally overnight) to allow the flavours to meld. Reheat and add the kale at this stage so that it stays bright green.
➤ Adjust the seasoning – the soup should be gentle, balanced, lightly creamy and deeply savoury. The Dulse adds a deep umami note to the soup, but it should not be a distinct flavour of its own.

CHILLED ALARIA SOUP &

Hewan Stuckenbruck's recipe from Madhur Jaffrey's inspirational *World Vegetarian* brings a healing soup into the frame. A light, minerally soup with a delicate, savoury taste and just enough heat to wake up the palate.

Traditionally eaten in Korean drinking holes where the soup, rich in antioxidants, gives much needed sustenance. Similarly, it would keep you going if kept in a flask when there was no time to go out for lunch. This is pure nutrition with virtually no calories. Put simply, it should be a regular part of our diets.

SERVES 4–6

8g dried Alaria (or Wakame)
   (rehydrated for 5 minutes
   in warm water)
1 litre Vegetable Stock
   (see page 51)
1 clove of garlic
4 teaspoons soy sauce
¼ teaspoon sugar

1 teaspoon sesame oil
225g cucumber, peeled, deseeded
   and diced
5 tablespoons diced red pepper
1 teaspoon red wine vinegar
1 teaspoon finely chopped fresh
   red chilli

METHOD

➢ Squeeze the water out of the soaked seaweed, then chop coarsely.
➢ Put the vegetable stock, seaweed and garlic in a pan over a medium heat. Add the soy sauce, sugar and sesame oil. Stir to mix all the flavours together. Allow to cool.
➢ Add the cucumber, red pepper, vinegar and chilli. Cover and chill before eating.

NOTE

Alaria is high in antioxidants and has 10 times the calcium of milk. Cucumber is high in silica, promoting joint health.

MUSSEL, PEA AND SEAWEED BROTH

Nathan Outlaw uses seaweed regularly in his restaurants in Cornwall and London. This soup balances the salt with sweet, using the Kombu umami to build on the stock and push the flavour bar out to greater depths.

SERVES 4

2kg mussels, live and cleaned
2 shallots, chopped
400ml dry cider
800ml fish stock
4 tablespoons ground Kombu
    flakes
160g freshly podded peas

Cornish sea salt and freshly ground
    black pepper
juice of 1 lime
8 fresh basil leaves
80g fresh Sea lettuce
good-quality rapeseed oil, to
    drizzle

METHOD

➤ Wash the mussels and remove the hairy beard that is attached to one end. Discard any that are open and refuse to close when sharply tapped as they are dead. Also discard any with damaged shells.

➤ To make the broth, place a pan that has a well-fitting lid and is big enough to hold all the mussels onto a medium heat. Heat the pan and, when hot, add the mussels, shallots and cider, then place the lid on straightaway. Steam for 2 minutes until the mussels open up.

➤ Take a colander and place it over a bowl, then pour the contents of the pan into it, saving all the lovely mussel juices.

➤ Heat the fish stock and add the mussel juices and Kombu to it. Take the pan off the heat and let the Kombu infuse and the mussel juices settle for 30 minutes (any fragments of shell or sand will sink to the bottom). In the meantime, pick out the mussel meat from the shells and set aside.

➤ Very carefully strain off the fish stock and mussel juices into another pan, leaving the sediment and seaweed behind.

➤ Bring a pan of salted water to the boil, add the peas and cook for 2 minutes. Drain, then plunge them into iced water and when they are cold, if needs be, slip them from their skins. (If the peas are very young and tender this may not be necessary.)

➤ Bring the mussel juices and fish stock mixture to the boil. Taste and season with salt, if necessary, and freshly ground black pepper. Add the mussels, peas and lime juice and heat through gently.

➤ Just before serving, slice the basil. Share the Sea lettuce among the bowls, pour the broth with the mussels and peas over this evenly, then scatter over the basil and drizzle with a little rapeseed oil.

MISO SOUP 🍃

Miso soup is pure liquid nourishment and comfort. It is the Japanese equivalent of chicken soup or ham and lentil broth. Filling but with virtually no calories, this is a great way to get acquainted with seaweed. Umami savouriness is at work here to make you feel like you have come home and put your slippers on. The macrobiotic community believe this dish forms a union of air, earth and sea – all in a bowl.

SERVES 4–6

1 tablespoon rapeseed oil
1 large onion, finely chopped
1 thumb-size piece of fresh ginger, peeled
3 cloves of garlic
2 carrots
2.25 litres Dashi Stock (see page 49) or use 2 x 15cm

blades of dried Kombu cut into matchstick pieces and added to 2.25 litres water
1 tablespoon brown rice miso paste
1 large potato, peeled and sliced
¼ cabbage, finely shredded (cut along the lines of the leaves)

TO GARNISH:

spring onions, finely chopped
½ red pepper, finely chopped
a few sprinkles of dried Alaria (or Wakame)

METHOD

➢ Place a large saucepan on a medium-hot ring. Put the oil in the pan and, when hot, add the onion. Make sure it sautés on a medium to low heat – do not let it burn. When the onion has become translucent, add the ginger and garlic and sweat the garlic for a few minutes.

➢ Peel the carrots and, with each carrot placed on a chopping board, do a long V-cut with a sharp knife three times at equal distances around the carrot, so that when you chop it across the top you have a flower.

➢ Add the stock or water, including the miso paste mixed in with some of the stock. Add the potato and carrots. Heat the soup, making sure that it does not boil. Cook for about 15 minutes, then add the cabbage. Cook for another 10 minutes.

➤ Add the chopped spring onions, red pepper and dried Alaria, then
  serve.

NOTE
Alaria is rich in calcium, magnesium and potassium, which are all
needed for healthy bones and teeth.

Whole leaf Kombu (*page 13*).

Pearl barley and Shony tabbouleh (*page 101*).

Thai pork balls with Kombu and chilli (*page 107*).

Orange Wakame seaviche (*page 117*).

Spinach and toasted Shony ricotta balls (*page 120*).

Dulse popcorn with maple syrup (*page 121*).

Rare beef with salsa verde and Dulse slaw (*page 129*).

Dried brown and green seaweed flakes (*page 21*).

FETA, POMEGRANATE, QUINOA AND ALARIA SALAD 🌿

Middle-Eastern food is known for its intense flavours and carefully balanced mix of spices. For the next best thing to being in the market or souk, where it smells of toasted seeds and sun-ripened sweetness, choose dark red tomatoes and pomegranates when the seeds are at their darkest and juiciest (September to January in the northern hemisphere and March to May in the southern). I like using half lentils and half another grain to add textural variety. Alaria works well with the other sweet flavours and gives you some serious mineral-boosting back.

SERVES 6

75g quinoa

75g puy lentils

15cm blade of dried Kombu

5g Alaria (or Wakame)

5 ripe large beef tomatoes, finely diced

1 pomegranate, cut into quarters, keeping the seeds

a glug of good-quality rapeseed oil

200g feta or goat's cheese, cut into cubes

1 small red onion, finely chopped

a medium bunch of fresh parsley, coarsely chopped

a few torn fresh basil leaves, to decorate

FOR THE POMEGRANATE MOLASSES DRESSING:

1 clove of garlic, crushed

1 thumb-size piece of fresh ginger, peeled and finely chopped

juice of 1 lime

1 teaspoon pomegranate molasses

1 teaspoon honey

1 teaspoon Seaweed Essence (see page 54)

3 tablespoons good-quality rapeseed oil

METHOD

➤ Put the quinoa in a saucepan of cold water and bring to the boil. Simmer for about 10 minutes and drain.

➤ Rinse the lentils thoroughly and put them into a medium-sized saucepan with water to cover over a medium heat. Add the piece of dried Kombu to help soften the pulses. Cook for 10–15 minutes until soft, but still nutty to bite.

➤ While the grains are cooking, put the dried Alaria in a food processor and whizz for a minute until it is reduced to fine pieces (they will swell in the water). Tip the chopped Alaria into a bowl of warm water and rehydrate for 5 minutes, then squeeze excess water out and drain. Chop finely if there are uneven sized pieces and set aside.

➤ Dice the tomatoes, drain the grains and pour into a bowl. Cut the pomegranate into quarters and ease the seeds out of the skin making sure you leave the yellow pith behind. Mix into the grains, adding a glug of oil to stop the grains sticking together. Add in the feta cheese, chopped onion and parsley.

➤ To make the pomegranate molasses dressing, mix all the ingredients together.

➤ Decorate the salad with a few basil leaves and dress with the pomegranate molasses dressing.

NOTE

It takes 25 gallons of water to produce 1 pound of wheat, but around 2,500 gallons of water are needed to produce 1 pound of meat.[19] With the rise of flexitarianism (carnivorous vegetarians) and the growing popularity of festivals like Vegfest, which attracts millions of people in the UK, consumers are more interested than ever in the ethics surrounding meat supply and environmental considerations. If we are to rely on more plant-based diets, seaweed has an important part to play in providing us with vital nutrients.

PEARL BARLEY AND SHONY TABBOULEH 🐝

When I first ate tabbouleh I could not believe how much flavour was
packed into what appeared to be a simple salad with few ingredients.
The seaweed-flavoured seeds take the salad one step further in terms of
complexity and I think it works well. There's a lot going on here.
Surprisingly filling, this could be a whole meal, or a good accompaniment
to chicken, salmon or falafels (see page 116). The nuttiness of the barley
goes superbly well with the toasted seaweed seeds.

SERVES 4

50g pearl barley

a generous glug of good-quality
   olive oil

50g cashew or pistachio nuts

1 tablespoon Shony flakes

1 teaspoon coriander seeds

1 teaspoon cumin seeds

80g fresh flat-leaf parsley

80g fresh mint

6 spring onions

¼ cucumber, diced into 1cm cubes

10 cherry tomatoes, halved

juice of 2 limes

1 teaspoon allspice

3 cloves of garlic, minced

METHOD

➤ Submerge your pearl barley in water and boil for 30 to 35 minutes
   until tender. Drain and set aside and, while still warm, pour over a
   generous glug of olive oil.

➤ Toast the nuts, seaweed and spices in a medium-hot dry frying pan
   until they turn pale golden and aromatic. Crush them all in a pestle
   and mortar. Add the nuts and spiced seeds to the tabbouleh.

➤ Finely slice your parsley leaves and stems, mint and spring onions. Add
   to your salad along with the cucumber and tomatoes. Mix together
   with your pearl barley, and finally, add your lime juice, allspice and
   garlic cloves.

SOUPS AND SALADS

TERIYAKI SALMON SALAD WITH NOODLES

Salmon and Dulse are a successful double act. With salmon more often than not being farmed, the seaweed adds a bona fide wild element, and healthy salt too. No salty nam pla fish sauce here! This is good, locally sourced umami. Make sure you source your salmon from a responsible supplier. (See list of suppliers page 172).

SERVES 4

4 salmon fillets (responsibly
    farmed and organic-certified)
1 teaspoon sesame oil
5 spring onions, finely sliced
120g mangetout
2 teaspoons sesame seeds

1 tablespoon Seaweed Essence
    (see page 54)
120g medium noodles
a small bunch of fresh coriander,
    roughly chopped
juice of 1 lime

FOR THE TERIYAKI SAUCE:
1 tablespoon clear honey
1 clove of garlic, crushed
1 teaspoon ground ginger
1 tablespoon Dulse flakes

METHOD

➤ Preheat the oven to 180°C/Gas 4.
➤ Put the salmon fillets on a baking tray lined with foil. Warm the teriyaki sauce until it thickens, then brush over the salmon fillets. Put in the fridge with cling film over the tray. Marinate for 15 minutes.
➤ Bake the salmon for 10 minutes until the flesh is opaque. Leave to cool, then remove from the skin and flake.
➤ In a wok, heat the sesame oil. Sauté the onions, mangetout and sesame seeds for a few minutes. Add the Seaweed Essence as you stir in the noodles for a few minutes, until they become soft.
➤ Take off the heat and add the flaked salmon flesh. Season with the chopped coriander and add the lime juice for extra zing.

NOTE
Salmon and seaweed both contain selenium, a powerful antioxidant that protects against cancer, detoxifying the body and promoting a healthy heart.

CELERIAC, GREEN APPLE, DULSE AND RED CABBAGE WARM ASIAN SLAW WITH TOASTED CRUSHED SOY ALMONDS ✿

This makes for an unusual slaw, particularly as it is warm and filling enough so you barely need anything to accompany it. It is a well-balanced dish with sweet and salt and a bit of sour, and an overriding umami loveliness.

SERVES 4

⅓ red cabbage
½ celeriac
2 cloves of garlic, thinly sliced
good-quality olive oil
2 tablespoons dried Dulse (ground)
2 green apples
juice of 2 limes
a large bunch of fresh coriander
50g almonds
1 teaspoon Seaweed Essence/soy sauce

METHOD

➤ Cut the red cabbage and celeriac into long thin matchsticks and fry with the garlic in some olive oil. Sprinkle over your Dulse and cook for 6 minutes – the cabbage should still retain a slight crunch. Put the cabbage and celeriac into a bowl. Chop your apples into matchsticks and pour the lime juice over them. Finely slice your coriander and add to the apple with a glug of olive oil. Add to the bowl with the cabbage, mix and toss together.

➤ Place the almonds in a frying pan over a medium heat and splash over your Seaweed Essence/soy sauce. It will completely reduce down to a black sticky coating over them. Toast for a few minutes but be careful not to let them burn. Roughly crush the nuts in a pestle and mortar and sprinkle over your slaw. Serve.

NOTE
Weight for weight there is more iron in Dulse and Sea lettuce than in sirloin steak.

SMALL DISHES AND LIGHT BITES

THAI PORK BALLS WITH KOMBU AND CHILLI

This dish won't last long on the table with hordes of appreciative teenagers around. I have tried this recipe with and without Kombu and there is no question that Kombu and pork bring out the best in each other. The light citrus notes of the herbs contrast beautifully with the umami, savoury flavours of the pork and seaweed. Perfect with noodles, but equally the meatballs can be eaten out of crisp salad leaves dipped in the chilli sauce, or in a vegetable broth, depending on the mood.

SERVES 4

a small bunch of fresh coriander (plus stalks)

a small bunch of fresh mint

a small bunch of fresh basil

400g good-quality pork mince

1 tablespoon Kombu flakes

2 fresh red chillies, deseeded and finely chopped

2 cloves of garlic, finely chopped

½ stalk lemongrass, finely chopped

4 tablespoons groundnut oil

3 baby gems or iceberg lettuce, to serve

FOR THE DIPPING SAUCE:

2 tablespoons Seaweed Essence (see page 54)

2 tablespoons sweet chilli sauce

METHOD

➤ Take the bunches of herbs, chop the toughest ends of the stalks off and put in a food processor. Mix until finely chopped.

➤ Put the pork mince in a medium mixing bowl and sprinkle the meat with the Kombu. Add the herbs, chilli, garlic and lemongrass. Mix thoroughly with your hands and form into golf ball-sized patties.

➤ Heat the oil in a heavy-based frying pan. Fry the balls, jiggling them as you go to make sure they are cooked uniformly.

➤ Combine the Seaweed Essence and chilli sauce in a bowl for the dipping sauce and serve with the meatballs and lettuce leaves to wrap.

SMALL DISHES AND LIGHT BITES

TRICOLORE OF LAND AND SEA ✿

It is hard to believe that this perfect pasta-shaped seaweed is not made from durum wheat or rice, such is nature's cleverness. Mixed in with courgetti and carrots, you have a natural trinity. Sea Spaghetti really scores on the health front too, iodine-rich and packed with minerals. This is literally a revelation to those tired of living in a pasta-based universe.

SERVES 4–6

300g dried Sea spaghetti (rehydrated for 5 minutes in warm water)

150g courgettes, spiralized

150g carrots (medium sized), spiralized

3 tablespoons groundnut oil

2 cloves of garlic, crushed

1 thumb-size piece of fresh ginger (peeled and chopped)

200ml Vegetable Stock (see page 51)

2 teaspoons Dulse flakes, to sprinkle

METHOD

➤ When it has rehydrated, rinse the Sea spaghetti in fresh water. Do this process four times. In a large pan of vegetable stock, cook the Sea spaghetti for 1 hour until soft. It should still have a little nuttiness to bite.

➤ Keeping the skins on the courgettes (good colour), spiralize them and the carrots. A tip here – smaller courgettes are easier to spiralize.

➤ Put a large wok on a very hot ring and heat up the oil. Fry the garlic and ginger until soft. Add the Sea spaghetti and make sure they are mixed round well for 5 minutes. Toss in the carrots and courgetti and mix the three coloured strands so they are intermingled in a lovely fusion of land and sea. Cook through until just soft – this will take about 5 minutes.

➤ Remove from the heat and serve a nest of noodles with sliced chicken or duck breast (see page 137) or with a dollop of pesto (see page 74) and don't forget to sprinkle over the Dulse to add a final flourish. Ta-da!

NOTE

Sea spaghetti has good levels of antioxidants such as vitamin C and can easily be eaten as a gluten-free alternative to spaghetti.

LIFE-SAVER SEAWEED RICE

If all you have in the cupboard is rice and a bag of dried seaweed, this could get you through such a moment. A bowl of this with a sprinkle of soy sauce is both comforting and nutritious. It is a favourite of my son, whose default position is to reach for the local take-away menu. I feel grateful that some things are finally getting through to him.

SERVES 4

5g dried whole leaf Alaria (or Wakame)

5g dried whole leaf Dulse

600ml water

2 tablespoons rapeseed oil

½ onion, finely chopped

2 cloves of garlic, chopped

200g basmati rice

a knob of butter

a handful of chopped fresh parsley

METHOD

➤ Soak the seaweed in the 600ml water for 5 to 10 minutes, then drain, making sure you keep the water, and chop the seaweed finely.

➤ Heat the oil in a medium heavy-based saucepan on a hot ring. First add the onion, turn the heat down and sauté for 5 minutes. Throw in the garlic and stir until softened. Add the seaweed and rice and stir the mixture. Add the water and turn the heat up. When it begins to boil, turn it down to a gentle simmer and cook for about 15 minutes or until the rice is cooked, preferably retaining its nuttiness, and all the water is absorbed.

➤ Remove from the heat and add a knob of butter for extra silkiness. Add the parsley and eat.

NOTE

Seaweed is a rich source of soluble fibre, which is good for our digestive system as it slows down the absorption of cholesterol and sugars. One 8g serving of seaweed can provide up to 12.5% of a person's daily fibre needs.

FRENCH TOAST WITH DULSE (SEAWEED EGGY BREAD)

This had to be in my comfort food section as I love the pure reassurance that the fusion of egg, bread (and seaweed) brings. The maple syrup drizzled over the top and the bacon rashers on the side are optional, but they really add to the overall union of this dish.

The fact that Dulse has bacon notes only adds to the moreish taste of this dish. More smoke, more flavour.

SERVES 1–2

2 pieces of bread, white or brown

2 large free-range eggs (beaten)

2 teaspoons Dulse flakes

2 teaspoons butter

2 teaspoons rapeseed oil

4 rashers of bacon (optional)

2 teaspoons maple syrup (optional)

METHOD

➤ Pour the egg into a flat-bottomed dish and place the slices of bread on top. Let the egg soak into the bread, this will take at least half an hour. Scatter half the Dulse over the eggy bread. Turn the bread over and soak the other side for the same amount of time. Scatter a bit more Dulse over the other side.

➤ Melt the butter and oil in a large heavy-based frying pan. When it is about to sizzle, drop the eggy bread pieces into the pan. If cooking bacon, put it in the pan and start cooking.

➤ Fry the eggy bread for a couple of minutes until golden brown. Flip over and cook the other side. Remove from the heat and put on two clean plates with the bacon.

➤ Drizzle with maple syrup if you want a sweet element.

EASY PIZZA

This recipe is a revelation. You really can make this pizza at home quicker than you can order it. Generously laden with as many toppings as you care to put on, it is nutritious and healthy with few calories. Make it vegetarian or meat, catering for all the different needs within your family. Pile it up with whatever is in season; if there's no rocket use kale, or make a smoked salmon-based pizza with capers, egg and dill. Seaweed here is used like a spice, adding flavour and goodness.

MAKES 2 X 25CM PIZZAS

375g plain flour (this can be gluten-free flour)

7g sachet dried yeast

1 tablespoon caster sugar

1 teaspoon dried rosemary

½ tablespoon Shony flakes (or Kombu flakes)

2 tablespoons good-quality olive oil

225ml warm water

500g passata

1 tablespoon Dulse flakes

FOR THE TOPPINGS:

140g mozzarella, sliced

1 avocado, sliced

70g pack of rocket

6 slices of Parma ham

10 cherry tomatoes, halved

good-quality olive oil

balsamic vinegar

METHOD

➤ Preheat the oven to 220°C/Gas 7.

➤ Put the flour, yeast, sugar, rosemary and seaweed in a large bowl. Mix in the oil and add the warm water until the dough is firm but not too sticky. Tip onto a work surface and knead until it comes together.

➤ Halve the dough and roll into two cylindrical shapes. If cooking separately, put one in the fridge wrapped in cling film. If making together, roll out into thin 25cm circles and place on a lightly oiled baking sheet.

➤ Spread the passata over each piece of dough, almost to the edge. Sprinkle the Dulse seaweed over the topping. Leave to stand for 15 minutes.

➤ Bake in the oven for 12 to 15 minutes until the dough is cooked golden. Remove from the oven and eat warm.
➤ You can either dress each pizza or put toppings on the table and people can individually do their own. Win, win.

> **NOTE**
> No other unprocessed, raw, organic material is known to contain more free MSG than Kombu seaweed.

EGGS FLORENTINE WITH SMOKED DULSE HOLLANDAISE 🌿

This is a good brunch or early supper option, when you need food that is reassuring and life-affirming. The golden yolks sit in a pool of smoky hollandaise like film stars, with a soft bed of iron-rich spinach beneath them. Mineral-boosting seaweed will sort you out: filling without being too rich. So what does the seaweed add? A bit of smoulder and smoke.

SERVES 2–4

a knob of butter, plus extra for buttering
250g spinach leaves
a pinch of nutmeg
1 teaspoon white wine vinegar
4 eggs, shelled
2 slices of toast
Smoked Dulse hollandaise (see page 71)
1 teaspoon Shony flakes

METHOD

➤ Melt the butter in a medium saucepan, add the spinach and nutmeg and heat through for a few minutes until wilted. Set aside.
➤ Put a medium saucepan half-filled with water on to boil. When you have brought it to the boil, add the vinegar and whisk the water. Drop the eggs in and take off the heat. Put a lid on and leave for 5 minutes until the whites are firm and have become opaque.
➤ Toast your bread, butter, halve and lay out on plates. Top with the warm spinach followed by the poached eggs, lifted out with a slotted spoon and drained on kitchen paper. Pour on a few spoonfuls of creamy smoked Dulse hollandaise.
➤ Sprinkle with Shony and serve. Help is at hand.

COMMANDER WALL'S POTTED SHRIMPS

Simon managed to get the White's Club's potted shrimps recipe from the Head Chef after a particularly memorable lunch there, dining with the head of the food committee. His idea was to replicate it at home and their secret, as we now know, was a dash of anchovy paste. Naturally, we had to do a head-to-head between the original and a new version with Dulse in. There is just the right amount of heat in this dish. There is also just the right amount of seaweed. The result is something classic with a twist of modernity.

SERVES 8–10

125g butter
¼ teaspoon ground ginger
¼ teaspoon cayenne pepper
¼ teaspoon ground mace
¼ teaspoon nutmeg
a dash of Tabasco

1½ heaped tablespoons Dulse
   flakes
1 pint peeled brown shrimps
lemon juice
freshly ground black pepper

METHOD

➢ Melt the butter in a medium-sized saucepan with the spices, Tabasco and seaweed. Add in the shrimps and stir well to distribute the flavours evenly. Squeeze lemon juice and grind some black pepper over them and check the spices.

➢ Scoop the shrimps into ramekin dishes, half filling each one. Pour the butter at the bottom of the pan into each dish and allow to solidify. Cool in the fridge.

NOTE
Seaweed starch consists largely of substances called algins, which soothe the digestive tract and give one the feeling of having eaten more.

SEAWEED FALAFELS 🌿

This is a quick-and-easy lunch or dinner solution, which is healthy and delicious too. What I like about the seaweed in the falafel is that it adds good nutrition and salt, so the whole thing is better. You can make a batch and keep in the fridge to eat after work, or in the evening as a companion to pre-dinner drinks. Stuff a few into a pitta bread with chopped-up salad, tomato and hummus and you have a substantial filler.

SERVES 4

2 x 400g tins of chickpeas
2 tablespoons Shony flakes
3 cloves of garlic
2 teaspoons ground coriander
1 teaspoon ground cumin
1 fresh green chilli, deseeded
1 small red onion, chopped

2 tablespoons tahini
1 tablespoon plain flour (gluten-free
   works just as well)
1 egg
50ml water
a small bunch of fresh parsley
3 tablespoons rapeseed oil

METHOD

➤ Drain the chickpeas and put into a food processor. Add all the other ingredients except the oil.
➤ Pulse briefly for 30 seconds – it is important that the mixture is not too smooth. If too dry, add some water and blitz for a few more seconds.
➤ Remove from the food processor and shape into small round patties the size of golf balls.
➤ Heat the oil in a heavy-based frying pan until very hot. Drop in the falafels and cook for approximately 2 to 3 minutes until they are golden brown all over. Remove from the pan and drain on kitchen paper.

NOTE
Traditional Chinese medicine includes Kombu (*Laminaria*) in the treatment of cancer. The ability of seaweed to chelate metals could help guard against cancers.

ORANGE WAKAME SEAVICHE

This dish was the highlight of a West Coast holiday. I had time to work the beach while harvesting at low tide and found beautiful young Alaria growing in stunning crystal-clear Atlantic water. This dish showcases the tender Alaria (Wakame), more commonly seen in miso soup, with local scallops bought from Mallaig. This dish will always represent the beauty and wildness of the Scottish Highlands to me.

SERVES 4

500g scallops (ask for hand-dived), seabass, mackerel or squid will do equally well

7 tablespoons fresh orange juice

2 tablespoons cider vinegar

zest of 1 orange

½ teaspoon ground cumin

5g dried Alaria (or Wakame), chopped

1 small red onion, thinly sliced

1 avocado, peeled, stone removed and chopped into 2cm cubes

a small bunch of fresh coriander, chopped

1 small fresh green chilli, deseeded and finely chopped

METHOD

➤ Make sure that your fish or seafood is as fresh as possible. If using scallops use a sharp knife and a steady hand, slice each scallop horizontally into thin circles (each one should do about three). Set aside.

➤ Mix together half the orange juice, the vinegar, zest and cumin and pour over the scallops. Toss in the liquid and add the Alaria pieces. Cover with cling film and put in the fridge overnight.

➤ Drain the fluid from the mixture and add the rest of the orange juice. Add the onion, avocado, coriander and chilli and mix around so that the flavours infuse thoroughly.

➤ Check the seasoning and serve.

SMALL DISHES AND LIGHT BITES

CURED MACKEREL FILLETS

I spent a few days on the West Coast of Scotland in July, just after the mackerel had swum up into the Sound of Mull. I showed cookery writer and gardener Sarah Raven how to identify the different types of seaweeds that grow near her cottage and together we came up with recipe ideas incorporating seaweed, which she then featured in her column. It was a lot of fun. It seemed completely right to be curing the mackerel (that we caught) with Kombu, rather than just traditional sea salt. This gave the fillets added flavour and we were making use of a local resource while we were at it.

SERVES 4–6

2 tablespoons rock salt

2 tablespoons demerara sugar

50g Kombu flakes

4 very fresh, responsibly sourced medium mackerel fillets

1 bay leaf

a sprig of fresh thyme

a pinch of peppercorns

juice of 1 lemon

6 tablespoons good-quality olive oil

DULSE MUSTARD

3 tablespoons Dijon mustard

1 tablespoon Dulse flakes

1 generous teaspoon honey

METHOD

➤ Combine the salt, sugar and seaweed so they are evenly mixed.

➤ Pour the mixture onto the bottom of a tray and lay the mackerel on top, flesh-side down.

➤ Cover with cling film and put in the fridge for 2 hours, turning a couple of times.

➤ Take the fish out of the fridge and drain the juices. Pat them dry with some kitchen paper. Lay a large, clean piece of cling film on a work surface and lay out the mackerel, skin-side down. Squeeze over the lemon juice, scatter over the bay leaf, thyme and peppercorns and pour the olive oil over them. Lay them in pairs, flesh on flesh, so they look like two whole fish. Wrap the cling film over them and tie the ends. Leave in a cool place for 6 hours.

➤ Remove the fish from the cool place and put a pan of water on the hob to boil. Plunge the wrapped mackerel in the water for 1 minute to blanch, remove, then immediately plunge into ice-cold water. This will stop the cooking process. Keep in the fridge until you want to eat them.

➤ We decided that the traditional dill sauce would overpower the subtle flavour of the cured mackerel. Dulse Mustard Sauce is the perfect alternative. This is self-sufficiency at its best!

NOTE

Red and green seaweeds are primarily composed of carbohydrates and provide a good energy source for the body, whilst brown seaweeds are high in fibre, which aids digestion, and iodine, which supports a healthy thyroid function and metabolism.

SPINACH AND TOASTED SHONY RICOTTA BALLS 🌿

These stunning balls of goodness are great for snacking on when mealtimes are a long way off. The golden nuttiness of the toasted seaweed contrasts with the creamy white ricotta and the crunch of the spinach. Serve with platters of cold meat or just with crunchy lettuce.

SERVES 2–4

1 tablespoon Shony flakes

125g ricotta

60g spinach, chopped very finely

125g breadcrumbs

a pinch of grated nutmeg

a squeeze of lemon juice

METHOD

➤ Toast your Shony seaweed in a dry frying pan for 2 to 3 minutes on a medium-hot ring until golden.

➤ In a medium bowl, mix the ricotta with the spinach, breadcrumbs, toasted Shony, a pinch of nutmeg and a squeeze of lemon juice. Mix thoroughly, then form into little balls with your hands. Keep refrigerated.

NOTE

Seaweed can help clear up the skin as it is high in chlorophyll, which is a natural detoxifier.

DULSE POPCORN WITH MAPLE SYRUP 🦋

Designer popcorn is all the rage at the moment and it is not difficult to DIY. The maple syrup/Dulse combination adds just the right balance of sweet/salty. We always argue in our house about which is nicer. This is not just a compromise, it tastes delicious too.

MAKES A MEDIUM-SIZED BOWL

30g unsalted butter
1 tablespoon rapeseed oil
150g popcorn kernels
3 tablespoons maple syrup
2 teaspoons Dulse flakes

METHOD

➤ Put a large heavy-based saucepan on a medium to hot heat. Add 20g of the butter and the oil and melt.

➤ Add the popcorn and move it around in the butter and oil until evenly covered.

➤ Put a lid on and leave for a few minutes until you hear the first pop. Shoogle the pan around on the hob so that the corn moves; this way all the kernels will heat up and pop. Make sure you keep the lid firmly on. If it smells as if the corn might be burning, take off the heat and wait until the popping stops, then mix round with a wooden spoon to free up any pieces stuck on the bottom.

➤ When all the corn has popped, which should take about 5 minutes in total, remove from the heat.

➤ Heat up the remaining butter and the maple syrup in a small pan. When the butter has melted, remove from the heat and pour over the corn. Scatter the Dulse over the popcorn and mix round with a metal spoon. Put any extra popcorn in a sealed tub for later. I am guessing this may not happen.

SMALL DISHES AND LIGHT BITES

ELISABETH LUARD'S CHEESE SHORTBREADS WITH DULSE 🐝

I have always admired Elisabeth Luard for her love of family, flavour and food, which are central to life. She has always stayed true to things local and traditional, and gathered inspiration from around her. A self-confessed seaweed user, she has given me a recipe where she comments that 'peppery little specks of dried Dulse add umami-moreishness'. This is the classic Dutch recipe for cheese biscuits, with equal weights of cheese, butter and flour.

MAKES 50 SHORTBREADS

250g butter, diced
250g grated cheese (Parmesan and Cheddar mixed)
250g plain flour (unbleached for better flavour)
2 tablespoons Dulse flakes
1 teaspoon salt
1 egg yolk, to bind
a splash of water (optional)

METHOD

➤ Beat the butter with the cheese to soften it a little. I do this with the dough hook on an electric mixer.
➤ Work in the flour, seaweed and salt until the mixture forms lumps – don't overbeat. Work in the egg yolk so everything comes together as a firm dough ball. Cut the dough into four and roll each piece into a fat sausage. Wrap in cling film and leave for half an hour in a cool place to rest.
➤ Preheat the oven to 180°C/Gas 4. With a broad-bladed knife, slice the dough sausage into discs, the thickness of two one pound coins.
➤ Arrange the discs on as many baking trays as you need to spread them out, with a little room between each to allow for spreading. Bake for 12 to 15 minutes, till golden brown.
➤ Transfer to a rack to cool and crisp if not eaten warm from the oven – unthinkable!
➤ Store in an airtight tin and reheat for a minute or two to restore texture and flavour. They're very rich and buttery, and seaweed adds a gorgeous crunch.

MOOIE'S FLATBREAD 🌿

Mooie Scott is an inspirational yoga teacher who knows about living well and eating well. She showed me this simple recipe, which you can cook up at a moment's notice. This is a straight substitution here for salt with seaweed. If you want to up the quantity of seaweed, you could sprinkle a few toasted seeds and seaweed on top when the breads are formed.

MAKES 10–12 FLATBREADS

570ml warm water

7g sachet dried yeast

1 teaspoon sugar

90ml good-quality olive oil

750g strong bread flour (can be a gluten-free version)

2 teaspoons Kombu flakes

2 teaspoons Shony flakes, to sprinkle (optional)

2 teaspoons sesame seeds, to sprinkle (optional)

METHOD

➤ Mix about 30ml of the water with the dried yeast in a cup and leave to activate in a warm place. Once activated, mix together with the sugar, oil and rest of the water in a large jug.

➤ Add the flour and Kombu to an electric mixer and slowly add water till a soft dough is formed. Alternatively, place the flour and Kombu in a large bowl and make a well in the centre. Slowly add the water and knead.

➤ Cover the dough and leave for about 30 minutes to rise in a large bowl with a little olive oil. Cover with a tea towel. Toast your Shony and sesame seeds in a dry frying pan for 2 to 3 minutes on a medium-hot ring until golden.

➤ Roll out each flatbread in an oblong shape and scatter with the toasted seaweed and seeds, place in a heavy flat-bottomed pan over a high heat to cook – about 6 to 8 minutes, turning over halfway through. Wrap them in foil or a cloth when they are done to keep them warm.

NOTE

Kombu is rich in vitamin K, which is essential for the blood clotting that helps wounds heal properly and is important for building strong bones.

CORN ON THE COB WITH DULSE CHILLI AND LIME BUTTER 🌿

Corn on the cob always seems to hit the spot. I had to put a recipe in as it is my youngest son's favourite food and I remember loving it as a kid. Seaweed, corn dripping in butter, a dash of citrus – you got it!

SERVES 4–6

3 large corn on the cobs, halved
Dulse Butter with Chilli and Lime (see page 60), cut into six rounds

METHOD

➢ Wrap the cob halves in tin foil parcels and roast on a BBQ or in the oven for 20 minutes. Unwrap and finish off under the grill to get that barbecued taste. Rub the cobs with the citrus seaweed butter to serve.

MAINS

Feeding my family and friends with seaweed has been a source of great enjoyment, sometimes spiralling into pure mirth. It is a human instinct to be curious about what you are eating. In the past I have to admit to sometimes smuggling in seaweed as an undercover ingredient, spooning it into burgers, lasagne, stews, salads, fish pies and risottos.

As my family and friends have begun to understand the value of seaweed, I have added chopped seaweed into everyday dishes to give more texture, taste, nourishment and invariably to add a talking point. They have now got the idea that when it tastes extra delicious, it usually has seaweed in it.

The flavour combinations in this section come from different food traditions, some that have seaweed at the heart of their culture (Southeast Asia and the Far East) and some that haven't yet embraced a love of seaweed. Umami is a universal taste that is shared by everyone and experienced in different ways through dishes unique to particular cultures. This is about everyone having access to good tastes and food, sharing big flavours and big ideas.

RARE BEEF WITH SALSA VERDE AND DULSE SLAW

The origin of this is an Alastair Little recipe, which very foodie friends, the Brooks, introduced me to many years ago and has long since been one of my favourites. Knowing how well the umami laden beef would work with the glutamate rich Dulse I had to put the two together, creating the perfect union of surf and turf. The tenderized fillet marinaded in oils and umami rich seasoning results in a deeply succulent and flavoursome dish. The secret is to slice the meat really thinly. The piquant salsa verde and celeriac slaw with Dulse add texture as well as more flavour.

SERVES 4
700g/1.5lb fillet of beef
200ml good-quality rapeseed oil
2 tablespoons Seaweed Essence (see page 54) or tamari soy sauce
1 tablespoon Dulse flakes

METHOD
➤ Cut the beef into wafer thin slices, tenderize the meat with a wooden mallet and place in a bowl. Drizzle over the rapeseed oil and the Seaweed Essence or soy sauce and scatter with the Dulse flakes. This will get all the rich umami flavours working together and will infuse the beef with yet more taste. Leave to marinade in the fridge for a couple of hours, turning the meat over at least once during this time.
➤ Heat the oven to 200°C/Gas 6. Remove the meat from the fridge and lay the beef over a couple of baking trays, so there is no likelihood of overlapping slices. Cook for no more than 1 to 2 minutes.
➤ Serve warm with Salsa Verde (see page 76) or new potatoes and the Celeriac Slaw (see page 103).

NOTE
There is more iron in an 8g serving of dry Dulse than in 100g of raw sirloin steak.[20]

MAINS

WHITE BEAN AND SAUSAGE STEW WITH DULSE AIOLI

Pork and seaweed have a synergy where the flavour of the sausages is boosted considerably by the addition of Dulse. The umami flavours do their stuff here. The Dulse aioli adds a drop of luxury to what is traditionally a body-and-soul peasant dish.

SERVES 4

1 teaspoon cumin seeds

4 tablespoons rapeseed oil

8 good-quality sausages

3 large red onions

3 sticks of celery

a large pinch of sea salt

3 carrots

a large bunch of fresh coriander

1 x 400g tin of cannellini/butter beans

1 teaspoon chilli flakes

2 x 400g tins of tomatoes

2 teaspoons Dulse flakes

Aioli (see page 70)

freshly ground black pepper

METHOD

➢ Toast the cumin seeds in a large pan, then add the oil and let them sizzle. Slice the sausages into chunks and fry until nicely browned. Remove from the pan and set aside.

➢ Do not wash your pan, instead slice the onions and celery and add them to the sausage juices with a large pinch of salt. Grate the carrots and add them too, along with the coriander stalks (sliced finely). Cook for about 15 to 20 minutes until soft.

➢ Add the beans, chilli flakes, sausages and tinned tomatoes. Allow the stew to simmer for 30 to 45 minutes. Meanwhile, make the Dulse aioli.

➢ Serve the stew hot with fresh coriander leaves, a dollop of aioli and black pepper.

NOTE

Seaweed has been a staple of Japanese culture for over 10,000 years and today forms 10% of the average person's diet.

Monkfish kebabs with Sea lettuce (*page 142*).

Spaghetti vongole with Kombu (*page 144*).

Dried whole leaf Carragheen (*page 17*).

Lentil burgers with Dulse (*page 149*).

Shony chocolate and frozen fruit (*page 160*).

Raw chocolate brownies with Dulse (*page 163*).

Very moist black ginger and smoked Dulse molasses cake (*page 167*).

Kombu, lemon, cardamom salt chocolate discs (*page 168*).

CRISPY PORK BELLY WITH FENNEL AND KOMBU, APPLE CHUTNEY AND AIOLI SLAW IN WARM FLATBREADS

The most prized pork in the land is marsh-reared. This is a shortcut to getting a similar result – chuck in the seaweed for added umaminess. The Dulse aioli slaw adds a clever twist to a classic dish. Delicious. If you want to eat the pork belly on the beach or for a picnic, you can do the prepping at home and finish crisping the pork on a barbecue grill.

SERVES 4–6

1 tablespoon fennel seeds, ground	1 tablespoon lemon juice
1 tablespoon Kombu flakes	1 tablespoon sea salt
4 cloves of garlic, ground into a paste with 1 teaspoon salt	2 apples (quartered)
	4 onions (quartered)
1kg pork belly, skin on	1 tablespoon white wine or water
2 tablespoons good-quality olive oil	warmed pitta breads, to serve

FOR THE SLAW:

1 fennel bulb, cut into matchsticks
¼ red cabbage, cut into matchsticks
1 cucumber, cut into matchsticks
4 tablespoons Dulse Aioli (see page 70)

METHOD

➤ Preheat the oven to its highest temperature, 200°C/Gas 6 or hotter (the oven needs to be really hot to start with so that the pork skin can be blistered and the crackling form, ensuring tasty crispiness).

➤ Rub the fennel seeds, Kombu and garlic over the flesh side of the pork belly with some olive oil. Squeeze the juice of a lemon over it. Make sure the skin side is very dry, sprinkle some salt onto this side and leave for 20 minutes to dry further.

➤ Put the apple and onion chunks into a large roasting dish, drizzle over olive oil and place the pork belly on top skin side upwards. Put on the top shelf of the very hot oven.

➤ Cook for 20 minutes, then reduce the heat to 180°C/Gas 4 for about 2 hours. Add wine/water during cooking so the fatty juices don't burn.

➤ Make the slaw and the Aioli while the pork is cooking.
➤ When the pork is cooked, remove from the oven and leave to rest for 30 minutes. Mix the vegetables with the Dulse Aioli.
➤ When cool, cut into bite-size pieces and serve in a pitta bread with the slaw and the baked onion and apple.

MICHAEL SMITH'S BREAST OF LAMB WITH CRISP KALE AND DULSE CRUMBS

Chef Michael Smith, Loch Bay Seafood Restaurant, Isle of Skye, has used our seaweed in fancy banquets in Monaco and in Shirley Spears' Three Chimneys restaurant, where guests came from all over the world to sample his food. Seaweed is part of his so called 'armoury' in the kitchen.

SERVES 4

1 breast (flank) lamb, top skin removed, rolled and tied
salt and freshly ground black pepper
1 onion, roughly chopped
1 carrot, roughly chopped
1 stick of celery, roughly chopped
a sprig of rosemary or thyme, chopped

1 bottle of white wine (cheap)
200g curly kale
oil (any), for frying
100g stale bread, broken down into rough crumbs
1 tablespoon Dulse flakes
boiled new potatoes, to serve

METHOD

➤ Preheat the oven to 180°C/Gas 4.
➤ Generously season the lamb with salt and pepper, seal and colour all round in a hot oiled pan.
➤ Put the chopped vegetables and herbs into a small roasting dish. Place the lamb on top of the vegetables, pour in the wine and slowly cook for 2 to 3 hours, checking once or twice to see that the liquid has not evaporated and topping up with a little water, if needed.
➤ Once the meat is cooked and tender, allow to cool slightly. Strain off the juices into a small pan and reduce slightly to make a light gravy.
➤ While the lamb is cooking, break down the kale into smallish pieces, then shred with a sharp knife. In a broad-based saucepan, add a very little oil, then add the shredded kale. Place on the hob on a low heat, stir with a wooden spoon and begin to dry out the kale, stirring every 5 minutes or so.
➤ After around 30 to 40 minutes the kale should have shrunk down and become like crisp flakes. Remove and drain on kitchen paper. Repeat the process with the bread, using a little more oil than before and a slightly higher heat, until the crumbs are golden and crispy. Drain on kitchen paper.
➤ In a bowl, mix the crumbs, the kale and the seaweed flakes. Serve the lamb with boiled new potatoes, generously sprinkling over the kale crumbs.

LAMB KOFTAS WITH DULSE

The bolstering umami flavour that Dulse gives this dish makes it an enduring favourite. There is a real difference in taste according to when new lamb is in season and whether it is locally sourced and hung properly, or frozen and imported from across the world. Either way, the addition of seaweed really contributes to the success of the recipe. Good to pack inside pitta bread with spiced yoghurt and chopped herbs.

SERVES 4

500g minced lamb
1 teaspoon ground cumin
2 teaspoons ground coriander
a pinch of ground cinnamon
2 cloves of garlic, crushed
a small bunch of fresh mint, finely chopped
1 tablespoon Dulse flakes
Shony harissa (see page 52)

METHOD

➢ Make sure you rinse your hands first to stop the mince sticking to them. Mix the lamb, cumin, coriander, cinnamon, garlic, mint and seaweed together in a bowl.

➢ When you are confident that the ingredients are thoroughly mixed, form into eight cylindrical shapes, about 4cm x 5cm. When they are all vaguely uniform in shape, slide two onto each of four skewers (preferably metal; if wood make sure they have been soaked in water for a few hours).

➢ Put a very light coating of oil on a heavy-based griddle pan on a hot ring. Cook the skewers in the pan and keep turning them every 2 minutes or so for about 10 minutes until the koftas are golden and cooked right through.

➢ Serve with the Shony harissa.

GET WRAPPED: LAMB IN KOMBU

Food that is wrapped has an extra layer of mystery, be it en papillotte, with a palm leaf, foil or baking parchment. Kombu is natural packaging, keeping the juices in and the sand out (if you are on a beach that is), providing a slow-release salt preservative wrap. Towards the end of the process, the Kombu leaves can be removed to do a final charcoal toast. This can be cooked in the oven or, better still, outside over a grill on the beach with seagulls wheeling over your head.

SERVES 4–6
2kg lamb, butterflied
15 x 15cm blades of dried Kombu (or wide strips of Saccharina)
    (rehydrated for 5 minutes in warm water)
pitta breads, to serve
salad, to serve

FOR THE MARINADE:
3 cloves of garlic, crushed
2 teaspoons ground cinnamon
2 teaspoons ground cumin
1 tablespoon fresh thyme leaves
1 tablespoon Dulse flakes
1 lemon, quartered

FOR THE YOGHURT RELISH:
a handful of fresh mint, chopped
seeds of 1 pomegranate
a pinch of sea salt
250g natural yoghurt

METHOD
➤ Put the garlic, spices, thyme and Dulse with the de-pipped lemon into a food processor and blitz. Massage the paste all over the butterfly of lamb, inside and out, making sure the flesh is infused with the flavours. Lay the meat so the flesh is upwards. Cover with cling film and put in the fridge overnight.
➤ Preheat the oven to 200°C/Gas 6 or light an outdoor grill.

MAINS

➤ Remove the lamb from the fridge, drain and pat dry with kitchen paper. Cover with the strips of Kombu, securing each blade with a cocktail stick. This process sits somewhere between first aid and present wrapping. Make sure all the flesh is covered.

➤ Prepare the yoghurt relish by mixing the chopped mint, pomegranate seeds and a pinch of salt with the yoghurt.

➤ If cooking indoors, put the lamb on a baking tray and cook for 45 minutes to 1 hour. Remove the Kombu wrapping for the last 10 minutes to make sure the meat cooks thoroughly and crisps on the outside.

➤ If cooking outdoors on a grill, make sure the fire is hot. Keep turning the parcel of lamb so that it cooks evenly. When the Kombu wrapper becomes golden brown and starts to char (after about 20 minutes) remove and complete the final 10 minutes sizzle wrapperless.

➤ Warm the pitta breads in the oven or on the edge of the grill.

➤ Cut the lamb into strips and eat in the pitta bread with the yoghurt relish and salad.

NOTE

The iodine in the seaweed acts as a preservative. Nature's perfect wrapper.

DUCK BREASTS WITH SEAWEED SEASONING

Silvy of The Blackface Meat Company is a Renaissance Woman – she paints, sings, cooks and also sells game to high-end chefs. A fan of the circular economy she also sells art works made from game bird feathers. She brought some wild mallard into the city to prepare and cook for a friend's dinner. We came up with this recipe, which showcases feathers and fronds well. We cooked her duck three ways and this is just one that was simple and super-delicous. The seaweed salt adds an extra layer of depth to the marinade.

SERVES 4-6

4 duck breasts

1 teaspoon Kombu, Fennel and Lemon Salt (see page 65)

1 teaspoon Chinese 5 spice

100ml olive oil

50ml toasted sesame oil

METHOD

➤ Score the skin of the duck breasts with a sharp knife. Rub the Kombu salt and Chinese 5 spice into the skin. Lay in a bowl, cover with the oils and refrigerate for 2 hours before cooking.

➤ Preheat the oven to 200°C/Gas 6.

➤ When the oven is hot enough, remove the duck breasts and lay on a baking tray. Put in the oven for 10 to 15 minutes, making sure that the skin is crispy and golden and the flesh still pink. Remove and slice finely.

➤ Eat with Tricolore of Land and Sea (see page 108) or Watercress Kombu Purée (see page 73) and Mooie's Flatbread (see page 124).

> **NOTE**
> The World Health Organisation (WHO) estimates that 2 billion people globally have insufficient iodine in their diets.

CARDAMOM CHICKEN THIGHS WITH LEMON AND DULSE YOGHURT AND SHONY HARISSA

The salt of the Dulse and the aromatics of the spices in this dish give the chicken superb flavour. The Dulse in the yoghurt pushes through the fabulous umami factor.

SERVES 4

1 tablespoon cardamom pods
1 teaspoon cumin seeds
1 teaspoon coriander seeds
5 cloves of garlic, minced
juice of 2 lemons
salt and freshly ground black pepper
1 tablespoon good-quality olive oil
4 large chicken thighs/legs, skin on

50g almonds
300g yoghurt
2 tablespoons tahini
1 teaspoon Dulse flakes
2 lemon rinds (you can use a potato peeler to remove this in strips)
a small bunch of fresh parsley, finely chopped
Shony Harissa (see page 52), to serve
pilau rice, to serve

METHOD

➤ Toast half the cardamom, the cumin and coriander seeds, then pound in a pestle and mortar (removing the cardamom pod shells as you go) with the garlic and the juice of 1 lemon. Season and add a glug of olive oil. Smear this all over the chicken and massage in. Marinate for 30 minutes.

➤ Preheat the oven to 180°C/Gas 4.

➤ Bake the chicken for 15 minutes or until half cooked. Toast and pound the rest of the cardamom and the almonds (they can be roughly crushed), then in a large bowl combine with the yoghurt, tahini, Dulse, the remaining lemon juice and the lemon rinds. Pour this over the chicken thighs and return them to the oven for 10 more minutes.

➤ Serve with lots of fresh parsley and ground black pepper, Shony harissa and pilau rice.

MAINS

HUGH'S FOIL-BAKED FISH WITH SMOKED DULSE AND GARLIC

Hugh Fearnley-Whittingstall is a fan of produce that is local and sustainable. The smoky seaweed enhances the flavour of the fish perfectly. This recipe would work well on an open fire as well as at home. You would have to do all the wrapping at home and take the parcel to the beach (remembering to bring the foil home!).

SERVES 2-4 (DEPENDING ON THE SIZE OF THE FISH)

30–50g butter, depending on the size of your fish

sea salt and freshly ground black pepper

1–2 large cloves of garlic, finely chopped

2–3 heaped teaspoons smoked Dulse

1 whole sea bass, about 600g–1.2kg, descaled if necessary and gutted (it's fine to leave the head on)

½ glass of dry white wine

lemon juice

cooked potatoes and steamed greens, to serve

METHOD

➤ Preheat the oven to 190°C/Gas 5.

➤ Melt the butter gently over a low heat in a small pan. Take a sheet of foil large enough to wrap the fish completely and grease the dull side of the foil with a little of the melted butter. Scatter some salt and pepper in the centre of the foil where the fish will go.

➤ Return the pan of butter to a gentle heat and add the garlic. Let the garlic sizzle gently for a minute or two but don't let it colour. Add the smoked Dulse, stir well and sizzle for a minute more.

➤ Meanwhile, season the cavity of the fish well, then place it in the centre of the greased foil. Bring up the sides of the foil to surround but not cover the fish. Splash the white wine over the fish.

➤ Trickle the hot, garlicky, seaweedy butter all over the fish in the foil. Season the uppermost side of the fish well with salt and pepper and give it a good squeeze of lemon, then bring up the foil over the fish. Scrunch the edges of the foil together so the fish is completely sealed in a secure but baggy parcel.

➤ Transfer the foil parcel to a baking tray and bake for 25 minutes for a 600g fish, 35 minutes for a 1.2kg fish (or somewhere in between for anything in between!). To test that the fish is done, open the foil slightly near the head end and insert a knife into the thickest part of the fish, behind the head. The flesh should be opaque and pull easily from the bone. If it's not quite there yet, close up the parcel again and return the fish to the oven for a few more minutes.

➤ When the fish is cooked, bring it to the table in its foil parcel and open it up. Release the flesh from one side of the fish and serve onto warm plates, then turn the fish over and release the flesh from the other side. Trickle some of the buttery juices from the foil over each portion and tuck in. Simply cooked potatoes and some steamed greens are all the accompaniments you need.

TIPS

This simple cooking technique works with many other species too, including black bream, trout and large mackerel. Flatfish such as plaice, flounder and dover sole are also very good cooked this way.

If you have some nice fresh fillets, rather than a whole fish, you can cook them very simply in a pan with the same butter, garlic and seaweed flavours. Heat the butter in a non-stick frying pan over a medium heat until just starting to bubble. Add the garlic and seaweed, then season the fish fillets and add them to the pan, skin-side down. Sprinkle a splash of wine over the fillets (just a splash – not half a glass), then cook gently for a few minutes until the fillets are opaque nearly all the way through, basting them occasionally with the pan juices. Carefully flip them over and cook for another minute or so. Give the fish a squeeze of lemon and serve with the buttery pan juices.

MONKFISH KEBABS WITH SEA LETTUCE

This dish can be cooked in an oven or on the beach over a fire. There is nothing like the smell of food cooking outdoors to get your juices up. I like the fact that beautiful Sea lettuce, rich with chlorophyll, finally gets out of its rockpool and becomes useful. Not only does it keep the fish juicy, but it lends a subtle saltiness and, finally, you get to eat the wrapper.

MAKES 4-6 KEBABS

500g monkfish tails, cut into about 18 x 4cm squares

1 teaspoon Kombu flakes

20g dried whole leaf Sea lettuce (about 18 pieces, 6cm x 3cm each) rehydrated for 5 minutes in warm water

2 small red onions, cut into quarters

6 cherry tomatoes

good-quality olive oil, for coating

1 lemon, cut into quarters (to squeeze over the kebabs)

plain rice or a simple green salad, to serve

METHOD

➤ Preheat the oven to 200°C/Gas 6. Work out the order of each food you are skewering and start with the main star; in this case the monkfish.

➤ First, season the fish with the Kombu flakes. Wrap each piece of monkfish in a leaf of Sea lettuce and slide a monkfish parcel onto each of six kebab skewers (preferably metal; if wood make sure they have been soaked in water for a few hours).

➤ Pop a chunk of red onion on, then another piece of wrapped monkfish and then a cherry tomato. Finish with another wrapped piece of monkfish. Repeat on the other skewers.

➤ When you have finished assembling the skewers, brush with a thin coating of oil and place on the beach fire if out and about. If at home, cook on a baking tray in a hot oven for 10 to 15 minutes, or until the onion is translucent and the fish is opaque.

➤ Eat with plain rice or a simple green salad and lemon quarters to squeeze over.

GRILLED SEA BASS WITH TARRAGON, LEMON AND SHONY

I like the utter simplicity of this dish, which is the way it should be when you have a beautiful piece of fresh white fish.

SERVES 4

4 sea bass fillets (responsibly farmed)
1 tablespoon Shony flakes
20 tarragon leaves, stripped from a sprig
zest of ½ a lemon
3 cloves of garlic, roughly chopped
2 tablespoons rapeseed oil

METHOD

➤ Preheat the oven to 200°C/Gas 6.
➤ Place the fish fillets on a baking tray lined with baking paper.
➤ Sprinkle the fish evenly with the seaweed blend. Scatter over the tarragon leaves, lemon zest and garlic.
➤ Drizzle with the oil and place in the oven or under a hot grill for about 10 to 15 minutes until the flesh is opaque and firm to touch.
➤ Serve with Watercress Kombu Purée (see page 73) or Salsa Verde (see page 76) and steamed rice.

TIP

To make things even quicker, you could infuse a litre of good-quality oil with a blade of Kombu or Dulse. Try adding peppercorns and some land herbs too. The flavour just keeps on deepening. This is taste on tap.

NOTE

Nori contains a compound called taurine, which benefits the liver function and so can help to control blood cholesterol levels.

MAINS

143

SPAGHETTI VONGOLE WITH KOMBU

In the early days when I was experimenting with seaweed, this was one of the first dishes that I cooked. No swanks, but it went down as a memorable one. The subtle but salty notes of the Kombu add more depth to the juices – which arguably are the best bit. This is a dish that will sell seaweed to even the most cynical.

SERVES 4-6

450g dried spaghetti
4 tablespoons good-quality
   rapeseed oil
1 medium onion, finely chopped
500g fresh clams
3 cloves of garlic
1 tablespoon dried Kombu,
   ground

1 red chilli, deseeded and finely
   chopped
250ml white wine
1 large bunch parsley, finely
   chopped
freshly ground black pepper

METHOD

➤ Cook your pasta in a pan of salted boiling water for approximately 10 to 15 minutes. Drain and return to the pan with a few tablespoons of oil. Put to one side while you make the sauce. In a large heavy-bottomed pan heat the oil and sauté the onion until translucent and soft, then add the clams, garlic, Kombu and chilli and cook for 1 minute before turning up the heat and adding the wine. The clams should be open now. Pick out and discard any that don't. Bring back to the boil, stirring gently, and add the spaghetti. Mix thoroughly and scatter on the parsley. Remember to mop up the juices with hunks of bread.

NOTE
If you use Kombu when cooking pasta, it can draw out the natural saltiness, so less salt needs to be added overall.

KEDGEREE WITH KOMBU

I first made this version of kedgeree after food critic friend Alex Renton recommended it. The rice and fish are cooked in the milk, thus the fish remains firm and fleshy. To this base I have added Kombu, which intensifies the flavour of the fish, and I have left out the curry powder as it has a big enough taste. This can be cooked at home or, if you like eating al fresco, transported to the beach.

SERVES 6

½ an onion, finely chopped
55g butter
300g basmati rice, rinsed
    thoroughly
1 tablespoon Kombu flakes
a pinch of nutmeg
200ml milk
110ml double cream

250ml water
300g smoked undyed haddock, cut
    into 3cm chunks
a knob of butter, to finish
a small bunch of fresh parsley,
    finely chopped
2 hard-boiled eggs, peeled and
    halved

METHOD

➤ Sauté the onion in the melted butter in a medium heavy-based pan over a low heat. When the onion becomes translucent, add the rice, continue to stir, then add the Kombu and nutmeg.

➤ Add the milk, cream and water. When the liquid is simmering, add the cubed fish and mix around, making sure that the rice doesn't stick to the bottom of the pan.

➤ Continue to stir until the rice has absorbed all the liquid. This should take about 20 minutes.

➤ Add more water if it looks too thick. The rice is ready when it has a slight nuttiness, but is beginning to soften.

➤ Finally, stir in a knob of butter, the chopped parsley and the eggs.

TIP

I like taking this dish to the beach in my wonderbag – a slow cooker that cooks by heat retention – and removing the lid to reveal a warming, soul-nourishing concoction of smoked fish and rice in a deliciously creamy sauce. No flames, no coals, no mess. Just hot food when you want it, whatever the season.

CASHEW NUT CURRY WITH KOMBU 🌿

Everyone loves a curry. This is easy and won't cost you too much in ingredients. It is creamy and succulent and fills you up without making you feel bloated. Not a hint of artificial MSG in sight, so less salt and bags of flavour.

SERVES 4

3 tablespoons rapeseed oil
1 onion, finely chopped
2 cloves of garlic, finely chopped
1 fresh red chilli, deseeded and
    finely chopped
2 teaspoons medium hot curry
    powder
1 teaspoon turmeric
1 teaspoon fenugreek seeds
6 fresh curry leaves (optional)
1 tablespoon Kombu flakes
100g cashew nuts (soaked for
    2 hours)

75g coconut milk, topped up to
    450ml with water
2 medium courgettes, chopped into
    small chunks
1 small cauliflower, cut into small
    florets
125g broccoli, cut into small florets
sea salt and freshly ground black
    pepper
juice of ½ lime
basmati rice, to serve
naan or flatbreads, to serve

METHOD

➤ Heat the oil in a large frying pan. Fry the onion, garlic, chilli, curry powder and other dry ingredients with the curry leaves and the Kombu for 5 minutes.

➤ Purée half the cashew nuts in a food processor and add them to the coconut milk.

➤ Pour the mix into the frying pan and combine by stirring thoroughly, then remove from the heat.

➤ Boil a pan of water and parboil the vegetables for 1 to 3 minutes. Drain them and immediately rinse with cold water to stop them cooking further.

➤ Add all the vegetables to the sauce and stir well, making sure the vegetables are fully submerged in the sauce. Simmer for approximately 4 minutes and remove from the heat.

➤ Check the seasoning and add a pinch of sea salt, if necessary. Add the lime juice and then the remaining whole nuts before serving with basmati rice and naan or another flatbread.

COURGETTI WITH SUMAC-ROASTED CHERRY TOMATOES, PINE NUTS, KALE AND SHONY 🌿

Producing your own long, twisting strands of vegetables doesn't take long and the results are so convincing that even those eating the dish might think this is the best pasta they have ever tasted. The seaweed blend adds just the right amount of salt and sweetness. This is a favourite of Sasha, who is sous-chefing at the moment and on her way up.

SERVES 4

15 cherry tomatoes

3 tablespoons good-quality olive oil

50g butter

2 whole bulbs of garlic

2 teaspoons sumac

2 fresh rosemary sprigs

20g light brown sugar

100g pine nuts

2 medium courgettes

1 tablespoon good-quality olive oil

2 tablespoons Shony flakes

3 large handfuls of curly kale

a splash of water

freshly ground pepper

1 tablespoon grated Parmesan cheese

METHOD

➤ Preheat the oven to 180°C/Gas 4.

➤ Put the cherry tomatoes on a baking tray and cover with olive oil, butter, the garlic (these can go in whole and be peeled when cooled), sumac, rosemary sprigs and brown sugar. Remove from the oven when completely soft, their skins are blistered and they are swimming in their delicious juices. About 5 minutes before they are ready, add the pine nuts. Be careful they don't burn.

➤ Meanwhile, spiralize the courgettes to make the courgetti. Squeeze the garlic from its skin – beware, this can be quite messy, you may want to wear rubber gloves. Heat some olive oil in a medium frying pan and add the sweet creamy roasted garlic and the Shony. Next add the courgette strands. Try not to stir too much; just fry for about 3 minutes, then stir for about 5 to 8 minutes until cooked through but still tender.

➤ Remove the courgetti from the pan and set aside in a bowl. Add the kale to the pan with a splash of water. Mix into the courgetti, along with the tomatoes and pine nuts, making sure you add all the succulent tomato juices.

➤ Serve with freshly ground pepper and a little grated Parmesan.

MAINS

LENTIL BURGERS WITH DULSE 🌿

For vegetarians it is important to have a burger option that tastes right. This is by far my favourite recipe for veggie burgers. Thanks to the Dulse there is a smoky, savoury deliciousness, which will have kids coming back for more. The melting cheese adds another layer of umami sweetness.

SERVES 4

1 medium sweet potato, peeled and roughly chopped

4 tablespoons rapeseed oil

2 cloves of garlic, crushed

3 spring onions, finely chopped

1 onion, finely chopped

1 tablespoon Dulse flakes

1 x 400g tin of brown lentils (or cooked Puy lentils)

120g hard mozzarella or sheep's milk cheese, grated (vegans can miss this out)

100g breadcrumbs (can be gluten-free)

1 fresh chilli, deseeded and finely chopped

a small bunch of fresh parsley, finely chopped

1 teaspoon ground cumin

1 egg, beaten

2 tablespoons plain flour (can be gluten-free)

1 tablespoon butter

wedges of lemon, to serve

steamed broccoli with Sea lettuce or Kale and Sea Lettuce Pesto with Walnuts (see page 74) on a bed of soft greens, to serve

METHOD

➤ First put a pan of water to boil on a medium-hot ring. Boil your sweet potato for 10 minutes until tender. Drain, mash and set aside.

➤ Meanwhile, heat half the oil in a frying pan and sauté the garlic, spring onions and onion. When translucent, add in the Dulse and lentils and stir for a few minutes so that all the flavours are absorbed. Transfer the mixture to a large mixing bowl with the sweet potato.

➤ Add the cheese, breadcrumbs, chilli, parsley and cumin. Add enough beaten egg to bind the mixture, but watch out it doesn't get too sticky.

➤ With your hands, form burger shapes and dust in flour. Don't worry if the mixture gets a bit tacky, it will harden in the fridge. Chill the burgers for 30 minutes.

➤ Remove the burgers from the fridge, preheat the oven to 200°C/Gas 6 and line a baking tray with greaseproof paper.

➤ Meanwhile, melt the butter and the rest of the oil in a hot frying pan. Cook the burgers on a medium heat on each side for approximately 5 minutes, watching that they do not burn. When golden on both top and bottom, transfer to the oven to be finished off for 5 minutes.

➤ Serve with a wedge of lemon, steamed broccoli with Sea lettuce, or Kale and Sea Lettuce Pesto with Walnuts on a bed of soft greens.

TIP

Add a strip of Kombu when you are cooking beans as the plant's glutamic acid will help to pre-digest them, which reduces the gas that can affect some people.

NOTE

The protein content of seaweeds can be as high as 47% of its dry weight.[21]

SPINACH AND GOAT'S CHEESE FRITTATA WITH DULSE 🌿

This is good, honest pan-fried food to warm your core. What is great about this dish is that it is easy to make seasonal adjustments. You could include nettles (blanched) in the spring, spinach in the autumn, or even young Dulse leaves in the summer. Here the sweetness of the goat's cheese blends well with the umami notes of the smoky Dulse. This went down well at a street market in West London, where the seaweed factor was what excited people, not the spinach.

SERVES 4–6

a small handful of spinach, roughly chopped

8 free-range eggs

4 spring onions, roughly chopped

zest of 1 unwaxed lemon

a pinch of nutmeg

2 tablespoons rapeseed oil

25g butter

1 tablespoon Dulse flakes

a handful of dried Dulse leaves (rehydrated in warm water for 5 minutes), finely chopped

150g goat's cheese

50g Parmesan cheese, grated

freshly ground black pepper

METHOD

➤ This is such a simple recipe that you could be watching TV or running a bath while you prepare it.

➤ Preheat the oven to 200°C/Gas 6.

➤ Put a pan of water on a medium-hot ring and bring to the boil. Blanch the spinach for about 30 seconds and with a spatula remove from the water and run cold water over it. Set aside. Break the eggs into a mixing bowl and beat with a whisk. Stir in the spring onions, lemon zest and nutmeg.

➤ In a large heavy-based ovenproof frying pan, heat the oil and butter. Pour in the egg mixture and cook for 2 to 5 minutes until it begins to set. Scatter the Dulse over the eggs evenly and do the same with the spinach. Crumble the goat's and Parmesan cheeses over the frittata and drizzle some oil over the top, add the black pepper. Put in the oven and cook for a few minutes until the cheese is melted and golden.

MAINS

MUSHROOM RISOTTO WITH KOMBU AND KALE ✿

This is a proper, building blocks type of risotto, which will make you feel
human again. The earthiness of the mushrooms and the mealiness of the
Kombu complement each other. Garlic is not required here as there is a
lot going on with the other flavours. The seaweed enriches this dish (don't
forget Kombu is Heston Blumenthal's secret weapon in his 'perfect'
chicken stock). The dark green of the kale adds contrast in terms of
colour and texture. If you can find a variety of different mushrooms it
adds more interest. Shitake and enoki mushrooms are fairly widely
available, but use whatever is in season.

SERVES 6

100g kale, chopped into strips
700g assorted mushrooms, chopped
   (wild, chestnut, shitake, enoki)
2 tablespoons good-quality olive oil
55g unsalted butter
1½ onions, finely chopped (red or
   white will do)
80g smoked bacon, finely chopped
1 litre good-quality chicken stock

480g arborio rice
1½ tablespoons Kombu flakes
1 large glass of dry white wine
a generous knob of butter, to finish
a large bunch of fresh parsley,
   chopped
a generous squeeze of lemon juice
sea salt
Parmesan cheese, to serve

METHOD

➤ Before you start the risotto you can cook the kale and get it out of the
   way. Heat a saucepan with water, enough to just cover the kale, put a
   lid on and bring it to the boil. Boil for 5 minutes, no longer, then take
   it off the heat. Drain in a colander, running cold water through it to
   stop it cooking. Drain again and set aside.

➤ Brush any dirt off the mushrooms and slice them finely if they are
   button mushrooms or chop into 2cm chunks if they are larger.

➤ It is important that when you start cooking the rice you are able to stir
   continuously for 15 minutes.

➤ Heat the olive oil and half the butter in a heavy-based saucepan over a
   medium heat. Sauté the onion, stirring constantly, until translucent.
   Add the bacon and allow to brown, but not burn.

➤ Meanwhile, warm the chicken stock through in a larger pan until it
   simmers gently.

➤ Add the arborio rice to the onion and coat thoroughly with the oil and butter. Spoon in the Kombu, making sure it coats the rice. This is a pure umami flavour bomb going in!

➤ Pour in the white wine and stir constantly. Ladle enough hot stock onto the rice mixture so that the rice is just covered, stirring all the time to stop it sticking to the bottom of the pan. Cook until the liquid is absorbed and repeat the process.

➤ After about 15 minutes, and just before you use up all the stock, the rice should taste nutty. Add the chopped mushrooms and stir well to make sure that they cook evenly. If necessary, put the lid on for a minute to create more heat.

➤ Stir in the final bit of stock, the kale and a generous knob of butter to stop the grains sticking together. Add the chopped parsley and, finally, check the seasoning. Add a generous squeeze of lemon juice and a small pinch of salt, if required.

➤ Eat immediately in large heated soup bowls. Grate large pieces of Parmesan over the risotto.

NOTE

Comparing Kombu with brown rice, the seaweed shows a higher level of fibre without containing much of the starchy carbohydrate that is present in brown rice.[22]

MAINS

PUDDINGS AND SWEET TREATS

Paul Hollywood (of *Bake Off* fame) was one of the first to recognize the affinity seaweed had with sweet tastes. On the BBC Show *Paul Hollywood's Pies & Puds* he selected Mara's Shony seaweed blend as one of his special ingredients, which he put into his perfect oat crumble. Oats, like seaweed, are a sustenance food, which look after you by giving you strength and nourishment. Iron-rich dark chocolate and Dulse also have a natural affinity with each other. Here are some ideas for some delicious puddings and cakes.

CASHEW NUT AND SHONY LEMON CHEESECAKE 🌿

Anu Sharma, nutritionist and acupuncturist, told me about her favourite pudding, which is not only delicious, but full of good nutrition. We discussed that the only thing missing was seaweed, which goes together so well with the nuts in the base. So this is the improved version. This is properly indulgent and nourishing, with no guilt attached. Just pleasure.

SERVES 6–8

FOR THE BASE:

135g macadamias, roasted

100g desiccated coconut (or fresh)

10 Medjool dates, pitted

15g coconut oil

2 teaspoons Shony flakes

FOR THE FILLING:

270g raw cashews

juice and zest of 3 lemons, plus extra zest to decorate

15g coconut cream

4 tablespoons maple syrup

15g coconut oil

METHOD

➤ Soak the cashews in water and leave for 5 hours.

➤ Add the macadamias, desiccated coconut, dates, coconut oil and seaweed to a food processor and whizz until fine and nicely combined.

➤ Take a greased springform tin and press the mixture firmly into the base to make a firm layer. Put this in the fridge to chill.

➤ Drain the cashews and add the lemon juice, lemon zest, coconut cream, maple syrup and coconut oil. Blitz in the food processor until you get a smooth and creamy consistency. It may take several minutes and several side scrapings to achieve a smooth result.

➤ Add the cashew mixture to the base and smooth it out. Garnish with some lemon zest and place in the fridge to set for 3 to 4 hours.

DULSE BANANA ICE CREAM 🌿

Bananas and Dulse are a great combination. Keep some bananas in your freezer for those moments when you want a cold shake, or to produce ice cream with no notice. The result? Creamy and luxurious, the salt of the Dulse complements the sweetness of the potassium-rich bananas, and so healthy. If you want some out-and-out decadence, add cream or at least serve some alongside in a jug.

SERVES 4

3 bananas
1 tablespoon flaked almonds
1 tablespoon maple syrup or honey
1 teaspoon vanilla pod seeds (cut the pod lengthways and
    scrape out with a teaspoon handle)
a pinch of ground cinnamon
2 teaspoons Dulse flakes
fresh berries and thick cream, to serve
a sprig of mint, to serve

FOR THE CHOCOLATE ALMOND BUTTER:

300g unsalted almonds
2 tablespoons Dulse flakes
100g chocolate chips
1 teaspoon vanilla extract
3 tablespoons olive oil

METHOD

➤ To make the chocolate almond butter, put the almonds into a food processor with the Dulse and mix until it forms first a flour, and then a butter, this may take a few minutes. Add the chocolate chips, the vanilla extract and enough oil to form a thick creamy spread. Remove from the processor and scoop the butter into a jar with a spatula. Keep in the fridge until needed.

➤ Peel the bananas and chop into large chunks. Put in a bag and leave in the freezer for 3 to 4 hours, depending on how cold your freezer is. Toast the almonds in a frying pan on a medium-hot ring until golden brown. Watch they don't burn.

➤ When the bananas are properly frozen, remove from the freezer and put in a blender with 1 tablespoon of the chocolate almond butter, the maple syrup, vanilla pod seeds, cinnamon and Dulse. Whizz for a few moments until thoroughly mixed. The ice cream should form into a thick, frozen mixture.

➤ Scoop out with a spatula into individual bowls and serve with fresh berries and a bowl of thick cream. Scatter the ice cream with the toasted almond flakes.

TIP

Maple syrup and honey can be good natural alternatives to sugar. Choose raw or Manuka honey.

SHONY CHOCOLATE AND FROZEN FRUIT 🌿

This is a winter fix. You've got a sugar low, are craving the sharpness of soft fruit and want to make a pudding with a sweet twist. This could be it. White chocolate and the tri-colour tutti frutti of the Shony blend go so well together. And it takes only minutes to prepare.

SERVES 4

200g good-quality white chocolate

2 tablespoons double cream

350g frozen berries (raspberries, blueberries, blackberries)

1 vanilla pod (cut the pod lengthways and scrape out the seeds with a teaspoon handle)

1 tablespoon Shony flakes

a sprig of fresh mint

METHOD

➢ Melt the chocolate approximately 10 minutes before you are going to eat. Put a glass bowl in a pan half-filled with water over a medium-hot heat. Bring the water to the boil, making sure the water is not touching the bowl. Break up the chocolate and place in the bowl. Melt the chocolate with the cream. When glossy and liquid, remove from the heat.

➢ While the chocolate is melting, lay your frozen fruit in a single layer in pudding bowls.

➢ When the chocolate and double cream has completely melted, add the vanilla and finally the flakes of seaweed. If there are any lumps, whisk the chocolate sauce until the consistency is smooth. Pour over the frozen fruit and serve immediately, with a sprig of mint.

NOTE

Mannitol (sugar) is often found in brown seaweeds, in particular the Kelps.

DAMSON CRANACHAN 🌿

Cranachan reminds me of skirling pipes, confetti and kilts. I had it at my wedding dinner as it was the most exotic pudding I had heard of. This version is unapologetically rich too. The seaweed stirred through the creamy oatmeal adds a touch of salty cheekiness to the proceedings. I warn you this is a party in a glass. Damsons are underrated and yet they have a sweetness and just the right amount of sharpness too. Other fruit will substitute, just go for whatever is seasonal.

SERVES 4

2 tablespoons medium oatmeal
300g fresh damsons (or raspberries, blueberries, whatever is available)
350ml double cream
2 tablespoons heather honey
1 teaspoon Shony flakes
2 tablespoons whisky or brandy

METHOD

➤ Preheat the oven to 200°C/Gas 6.
➤ Toast the oatmeal in the oven for 5 minutes until it is golden and smells nutty.
➤ Crush half the damsons with a fork and remove the stones, set aside.
➤ Whisk the double cream, making sure that it is not too thick. Mix in the oatmeal, honey, seaweed and alcohol.
➤ This will look pretty, so spoon the pudding into shallow champagne glasses, wine glasses or bowls, alternating layers of oatmeal cream with the purée and most of the remaining whole fruit.
➤ Scatter a dusting of Shony seaweed on top with the last of the whole fruit. Cool the puddings in the fridge before eating.

POWER BARS WITH SEAWEED 🐟

These don't just look good – they are good. They would be perfect to eat on a walk or bike ride or any time of the day when you have a sugar low (mid afternoon?). The great thing is that you can alter what you put into the bars according to what you like and what you have in your cupboard. I have used goji and chia seeds to get some nutritional super-charging going. I love the combination of seeds, oats, dried fruit and seaweed.

MAKES 12 BARS

200g dates

120g rolled oats

1 tablespoon chia seeds

1 tablespoon Shony flakes

1 teaspoon vanilla extract

1 tablespoon water (optional)

2 tablespoons clear honey

80g cashews

60g ground almonds

135g pistachios

80g dried apricots (non-sulphur ones)

a small handful of goji berries

METHOD

➢ Soak the dates for 30 minutes in water so that they are easier to process, then drain them and remove their stones.

➢ Put the dates, oats, chia seeds, seaweed and vanilla extract in a food processor and mix until a creamy consistency. Add a tablespoon of water, if necessary, so that it will not become stuck around the blade. Add the rest of the ingredients and blitz.

➢ Spread some baking paper in a baking tin and spread the mixture over the base with a large pallet knife, making sure that it is spread evenly and about 1.5cm deep ideally. Put in the freezer for 2 hours.

➢ When you remove the tray from the freezer, score the sweet block of deliciousness into squares of about 4cm.

NOTE

Mannitol (present in seaweed) is a sweet-tasting sugar alcohol that has about 60% of the sweetness of table sugar (sucrose).

RAW CHOCOLATE BROWNIES WITH DULSE 🥬

If you are going to use great ingredients there is an argument to say, why cook it? This recipe (inspired by the minimalistbaker.com) is uncooked, but still has the chocolate intensity that you look for in a brownie and is stacked full of nuts, seaweed and more nuts. No sugar or butter used here. You can genuinely enjoy a guilt-free snack, but get your fix of chocolate. The seaweed adds a superboost that you know is there, but there are many other toasted and roasted flavours coming through. It is really worth sourcing raw cacao for this treat. Raw is the future.

MAKES 16 SQUARES

60g almonds

60g pecans

100g rolled oats

135g walnuts

300g dates, pitted and soaked

135g raw cacao powder

1 tablespoon Dulse flakes

2 tablespoons maple syrup/honey

50g Chocolate Almond Butter
(see page 158) (or plain almond
or peanut butter if you don't
have time)

METHOD

➤ Preheat the oven to 200°C/Gas 6. Line a large baking tray with parchment paper.

➤ Toast the almonds, pecans and rolled oats in the oven for about 5 minutes until golden – be careful that you do not burn them.

➤ Mix the walnuts and dates in a food processor until they form a pulp. Add the cacao powder and Dulse and pulse for a few minutes until well mixed.

➤ Put the maple syrup and Chocolate Almond Butter in a small pan and warm through until liquid.

➤ Transfer the walnut and cacao mixture to the roasted nuts and oats. Add in the maple syrup and Chocolate Almond Butter to the mixture and incorporate well with a wooden spoon or your hands.

➤ The mixture will be quite heavy to handle. Press the mixture into the baking tray to a depth of 1cm, aiming for as even a level as possible. Put tin foil on top and press down again with a large spoon. Put in the fridge for 20 minutes before slicing up.

➤ Keep in a sealed tin. You will not be able to stay away from them for
long. You are warned.

NOTE
Raw cacao contains the minerals magnesium, iron and zinc and it is
high in antioxidants such as resveratrol, which helps to protect your
nervous system.

CHOCOLATE CAKE WITH DULSE 🍃

I tried the healthy way, cooking cakes with different exotic vegetable
species, but most of them ended up in the bin. Then I came back to a more
fudgy, indulgent one based on my favourite recipe. The introduction of
Dulse in the recipe instead of salt adds a drop of wholesomeness. The
iron-rich dark chocolate and Dulse act as great partners for each other.
There is a time and place for falling off the wagon of virtue – this is it!

SERVES 8

250g good-quality dark chocolate
250g unsalted butter
5 free-range eggs, separated
200g soft light brown sugar
100ml instant coffee
½ tablespoon Dulse flakes
1 teaspoon vanilla extract

METHOD

➤ Preheat the oven to 170°C/Gas 3. Grease a 23cm cake tin, preferably
  springform.
➤ Put the chocolate and butter in a bowl over a pan of simmering water,
  making sure that the water does not touch the base of the bowl. Stir
  periodically until the mixture has melted.
➤ In a large bowl, mix the egg yolks with the sugar to form a thick paste.
  Add the coffee and stir. Pour the melted chocolate and butter into the
  mixture and combine thoroughly. Add in the Dulse and vanilla extract.
➤ Whisk the egg whites until they form stiff peaks and stir 1 tablespoon
  into the chocolate mixture, then fold in the rest of the mixture with a
  metal spoon, making sure that you incorporate as much air as possible.
➤ Pour into the prepared cake tin and place on a baking tray. Bake in the
  oven for 35 to 40 minutes. The middle should still be slightly wobbly,
  but firm to touch on the top.
➤ Leave to cool for 15 minutes before taking out of the tin. Serve with
  raspberries and crème fraîche or cream.

NOTE
A little dark chocolate is good for you – it has high antioxidant levels
and minerals such as iron, magnesium, copper and manganese.

VERY MOIST BLACK GINGER AND SMOKED DULSE MOLASSES CAKE 🦐

Everyone loves a sticky gingerbread. This is in memory of summer holidays by the sea staying on the Moray Firth, where we wore sand shoes and ate off green melamine plates. Dulse fits brilliantly in here with sweet and complex flavours. I like to think it is adding a bit of goodness too.

SERVES 8

175g butter

100g molasses or treacle (about 3 tablespoons)

¾ tablespoon ground ginger

½ thumb-size piece of fresh ginger, peeled and grated

half jar of stem ginger in syrup (make sure you finely chop or process the chunks)

1 tablespoon Dulse flakes

½ teaspoon ground cinnamon

1 teaspoon baking powder

200g self-raising flour

2 free-range eggs, lightly beaten

160ml whole milk or cream

METHOD

➤ Utensils: large 2lb/900g loaf tin (25.75 x 12.75 x 6.75cm)

➤ Preheat the oven to 180°C/Gas 4.

➤ Melt the butter in a large saucepan very slowly until it just melts. Remove from the heat and add molasses, ground ginger, freshly grated ginger, the stem ginger and all of its syrup, Dulse, cinnamon, baking powder and the flour, in that order.

➤ Beat the eggs and stir into the mix. Finally add milk. A dark sloppy batter should be formed. Gently mix well.

➤ Line the large loaf tin with greaseproof paper and pour in your mix. Bake for 45 minutes. Serve hot, smothered in melting butter.

PUDDINGS AND SWEET TREATS

KOMBU, LEMON, CARDAMOM SALT
CHOCOLATE DISCS 🌿

If you have ever had any pretensions to being a master chocolatier, this is your moment to have a go. You could put your stopwatch on and have your presentation box of chocs ready in under an hour (including cooling time) Seriously.

MAKES 20 CHOCOLATE DISCS
100g good-quality dark chocolate
1 teaspoon Kombu, Fennel and Lemon Salt (see page 65)
2 teaspoons pistachio nuts, crushed roughly in a pestle and mortar

METHOD
➤ Put a glass bowl in a pan half-filled with water on a medium-hot ring. Bring the water to the boil, making sure the water is not touching the bowl. Break up a bar of dark chocolate and place in the bowl. Melt the chocolate. When glossy and liquid, remove from the heat.
➤ With a teaspoon, take a scoop and drop a round disc, almost like painting it, on a piece of baking paper. Do as many round blobs as you have chocolate. Take a pinch of Kombu salt between your fingers and scatter over the middle of the chocolate discs. Do the same with the crushed nuts. This will be the gorgeous exotic finishing touch to your chocolates. Work quickly because the chocolate will cool and set. Beautiful.

NOTE
This is a double present – iron-rich dark chocolate and iodine-rich Kombu.

COCONUT, CARROT AND SEAWEED LOAF 🌿

This recipe, shown me by Evie who used to work in the office, takes the theme of carrot cake and makes it so much more. Umami-rich Dulse works well with 'sweet' as well as savoury, while carrots are high in glutamates and are perfect partners for seaweed. Citrus also combines well with these flavours. There is a lot of interesting texture and colour in the cake with a good amount of dampness. The net result – it rendered our photographer speechless (not often the case) when after a long day trying to get the right shots, he was allowed a piece. Perfect with a cup of smoky Earl Grey.

SERVES 8

300ml light olive oil
115g dark brown sugar
3 free-range eggs
200g wholemeal flour
1 tablespoon Dulse flakes
1 teaspoon baking powder
1 teaspoon bicarbonate of soda

70g desiccated coconut
350g carrots, grated
100g pistachios, toasted and
    roughly chopped
4 cardamom seeds, ground
zest of 1 orange

TOPPING

4 tablespoons icing sugar
1 tablespoon lemon juice
1 tsp Dulse flakes
zest of 1 orange
Utensils: large 2lb/900g loaf tin (25.75 x 12.75 x 6.75cm)

METHOD

➤ Preheat the oven to 190°C/Gas 5. Oil your loaf tin.
➤ Mix the oil and sugar together in a large bowl with a wooden spoon. With a hand whisk, mix in the eggs one at a time.
➤ In another bowl, mix together the flour, Dulse, baking powder, bicarbonate of soda and coconut. With a large metal spoon, fold the flour mixture into the egg mixture.
➤ Add the carrot, pistachios, cardamom and orange zest and mix thoroughly.
➤ Pour into the oiled loaf tin and bake for 40 minutes. Take out, cover with tin foil and bake for a further 10 to 15 minutes.
➤ Decorate with icing sugar and the lemon juice mixed together to make a runny icing to dribble over the cake. Sprinkle Dulse and orange zest over the top.

THANKS

Firstly thanks to my literary agent Clare Hulton, commissioning editor Lindsey Evans and the team at Penguin, Michael Joseph, without which this project would not have got beyond the drawing board. Zoe has my gratitude for her superb editing skills. My thanks go to team Mara Seaweed, chairman Robin Worsnop, director Jim Fallon and CEO Fiona Houston who drives the operation, or should I say navigates, through often choppy waters, and in no particular order: Niall, Rory, Roddy, Lee, George Pike, Peter Farquhar, Duncan Wood, Anjeli Meta, Gail Turpin, Pawel, Callum Grieve, all at Luminous and Storm, colleagues past and present, who continue to believe in the shared dream and work hard to achieve it.

To all our community, which extends from friends, Sarah Raven, Adam Nicolson, Hugh Fearnley-Whittingstall and Adrian Gill who needed a little persuading, they are discerning after all, but have seen the potential in seaweed. To our favourite chefs and influencers who have tweeted and chirped about how delicious and fascinating seaweed is: Cyrus Todiwala, Paul Hollywood, Sheila Dillon et al.

Our business dovetails with the greater ambition for the people of Scotland to have greater access to good food that is locally grown, and the organizations Nourish and Slow Food who continue to champion small farmers and produce from around the world. Seaweed is a global food which could provide valuable nutrition in continents where food shortages are still an issue, i.e. Africa. This joined up thinking is important in terms of a fairer food system for all. Along with other small producers we want our product to be accessible in small outlets away from city centres.

Thank you to chefs Michael Smith, Roy Brett, Nathan Outlaw, Brett Graham, Paul Wedgwood, Carla Lamont and everyone who has contributed recipes, not all of which we have been able to include: Matt Fountain at the Freedom Bakery, Elaine Mason, Union of Genius, master chocolatier Sebastian Kobelt, Jason Scott, Cristina Lopez, Evie Dunne, Brambles Cocktail Bar, Reiko Hashimoto, Elisabeth Luard, Catherine Brown, Anu Sharma, Jamie Sawyer, Sue Appelboom, Kellie Anderson, Food to Glow, Rachel Meddowes, Lorna Crawfurd, Twist and Sprout.

To my friends who helped with ideas and provided a good sounding board: Jane Raven, Alice Stobart, Diana and Charlie McMicking, Anabel, Stephanie, Beeb, Silvy, Rob Beckett and Rosie Mackintosh, Natasha Morgan (for her 50th), Claudia Downes, Ruth and Davi, Melissa Fergusson, Merryn Somerset Webb, Ali Grant, Florence and Richard

Ingleby, Alex Renton, Mooie Scott, Fenella Douglas-Hamilton, Stephanie Frapier, Rachel and Willie Barne, Denis and Mindy Milne, Elizabeth, and my siblings, apologies to anyone I have forgotten – you know who you are.

Scotland and the wider UK are different places now, from when we started the business, all those original supporters know who they are: Tracey Crozier, Jennifer Bryson, QMU, Rowett Institute, Transition Scotland, Donald Reid, The List, Nourish, Slow Foodies and Scotland Food and Drink who have never stopped promoting us. Their endorsement is helping to push the message further out.

Thanks also to my long-suffering, but hopefully well-fed husband Simon, and my lovely boys Geordie, Lorne and Mungo; to wider family and friends for their enthusiasm, support and unerring humour. Special thanks go to talented and upcoming culinary star Sasha Scott for her huge creative input and support, thanks also to Imi Grant for her help when I really needed someone to organize me. Kerry Rae took on the role of nutritionist willingly and with an open heart, when I felt the book needed it. Catherine Labilowicz came on board despite her heavy workload. Not one of them hesitated when asked if they might join the seaweed project and they have all given up significant amounts of valuable time simply because they believe in the future of seaweed.

'We love it, but how do you use it?' has been a constant cry amongst the Mara community. This book is about redressing the balance. It is mostly about instinct – a pinch here, a spoonful there, a cut-up blade stirred into something. But ultimately it is about believing that seaweed in food DOES make a difference. We know it does. We hope you do too.

UK SEAWEED SUPPLIERS AND STOCKISTS:

These are just a few of the places selling premium fresh and dried sustainably sourced seaweed. Dried seaweed is light, so can be easily and quickly sent by mail.

Specialist:
- http://www.justseaweed.com
- https://www.seaweedheaven.uk/Producers
- http://cornishseaweed.co.uk
- http://maraseaweed.com
- http://atlantickitchen.co.uk
- http://www.pembrokeshirebeachfood.co.uk
- http://www.seaveg.co.uk
- http://www.emeraldisleseaweed.com
- http://wildirishseaveg.com/shop

General:
- Ocado.com
- Amazon.co.uk
- http://www.planetorganic.com
- https://www.hubbub.co.uk/
- http://www.inspiral.co/shop
- http://www.naturalgrocery.co.uk/Grocery/sustainable-fish-seaweed
- http://natuhealth.co.uk
- http://www.natureshealthbox.co.uk
- http://rawsuperfoods.com/en
- http://www.realfoods.co.uk/shop

UK Supermarkets:
- Asda
- Tesco
- Sainsbury's
- Lidl
- Aldi
- Marks & Spencer

In Store
London:
- Harrods
- Harvey Nichols
- Selfridges Food Hall

- Wholefoods Markets
- Planet Organic
- Portobello Wholefoods
- The People's Supermarket
- Budgens
- As Nature Intended
- Spar E9, Homerton
- Eat 17, Walthamstow
- Mother Earth, Highbury and Islington
- Gaia Wholefoods, Twickenham

Regional:
- Wild Oats, Bristol
- Harvey Nichols:
- Bristol
- Birmingham
- Manchester
- Leeds
- Liverpool
- Edinburgh
- Real Foods Edinburgh
- Earthy Edinburgh
- Wholefoods Market:
- Cheltenham
- Giffnock, Glasgow

Sustainable Food Suppliers:
  http://www.goodfishguide.org/
- Marine Conservation Society list of sustainable fish/suppliers:
  https://msc.org/where-to-buy/product-finder
- Marine Stewardship Council blue label:
  http://www.leafuk.org/leaf/foodchain/supplychaindirectory.aspx.eb
- Linking environment and farming:
  http://www.wedeliverlocal.co.uk/
- Regional food groups, part of a wider network called the English Food and Drink Alliance:
  www.englishfoodanddrinkalliance.co.uk

Shop at your local butcher, fishmonger, greengrocer and farm shop online:
https://www.rspcaassured.org.uk/where-to-buy/map/
https://www.bigbarn.co.uk/producers/
- Local producers in your area:
https://thefoodassembly.com/en

NOTES

Page 5: 1 M. Bell in: Brothwell, D. and Dimbleby, G. (1981). *Environmental aspects of coasts and islands.* Oxford, England: B.A.R.

Page 6: 2 Kelly, F. (1997). *Early Irish farming.* [Dublin]: School of Celtic Studies, Dublin Institute for Advanced Studies.

Page 6: 3 Brown, C. and Knowelden, M. (1990). *Broths to bannocks: Cooking in Scotland 1690 to the present day.* London: Murray.

Page 6: 4 Carmichael, A. (1941). *Carmina Gadelica: Hymns and incantations with illustrative notes on words, rites and customs, dying and obsolete: orally collected in the Highlands and Islands of Scotland,* vol. iv, pp. 32-3. Edinburgh: Scottish Acad. Press.

Page 9: 5 Sasano, T., Satoh-Kuriwoda, S. and Shoji, N. (2015). The important role of umami taste in oral and overall health. *Flavour,* 4 (10)

Page 9: 6 Hepburn, C. (2010). Market trends in human health and nutrition and how seaweed is responding. Cybercolloids Ltd report.

Page 9: 7 Hotchkiss, S. (2010). Investigation of the flavouring and taste components of Irish seaweeds. *Marine research Sub-Programme (NDP 2007-'13) Series.* Galway, Ireland: Marine Institute.

Page 10: 8 ibid. p. 1.

Page 10: 9 Sheffield Hallam University: Brownlee, Iain, Fairclough, Andrew Hall, Anna and Paxman, Jenny (2012) The Potential health benefits of seaweed and seaweed extract. In: Pomin, Vitor H, (ed) Seaweed: ecology, nutrient composition and medicinal uses. Marine Biology: Earth Sciences in the 21st Century. Hauppauge, New York Noval Science Publishers, 119-136.

Page 10: 10 Anthony, M., Blumenthal, H., Bourdas, A., Kinch, D., Martinez, V., Matsuhisa, N., Murata, Y., Schiaffino, M. (2014) *Umami: the fifth taste.* Tokyo: Japan Publications Trading Co.

Page 11: 11 Mouritsen, O.G., Williams, L., Bjerregaard, R. and Duelund L. (2012). Seaweeds for umami flavour in the new Nordic cuisine. *Flavour,* 1 (4)

Page 11: 12 Umami Information Center. http://www.umamiinfo.com/

Page 12:   13 Consensus Action on Salt & Health. http://www.actiononsalt.org.uk/

Page 12:   14 Gupta et al, 2010

Page 66:   15 Consensus Action on Salt & Health. http://www.actiononsalt.org. uk/news/surveys/2016/Hidden%20Salt%20Survey/171366.html

Page 85:   16 Aceves, C., Anguiano, B. and Delgado, G. (2005). Is iodine a gatekeeper of the integrity of the mammary gland? *Journal of Mammary Gland Biology and Neoplasia*, 10 (2), pp. 189-96.

Page 85:   17 Smyth, P.P. (2003). The thyroid, iodine and breast cancer. *Breast Cancer Research*, 5 (5), pp. 235-8.

Page 85:   18 Patrick, L. (2008). Iodine: deficiency and therapeutic considerations. *Alternative Medicine Review*, 13 (2), pp. 116-27.

Page 100:   19 Robbins, J. (1987). *Diet for a new America*. Walpole, NH: Stillpoint.

Page 129:   20 Institut de Phytonutrition (2004). Functional, Health and Therapeutic Effects of Algae and Seaweed. *Institut de Phytonutrition Electronic Database,* version 1.5. Beausoleil, France. Also: McCance, R.A., Widdowson, E.M. and Holland, B. (1993). *McCance and Widdowson's The composition of foods.* 6th edition. Cambridge: Royal Society of Chemistry.

Page 150:   21 Fleurence, J. (1999). Seaweed proteins: biochemical, nutritional aspects and potential uses. *Trends in Food Science & Technology*, 10, pp. 25-38.

Page 153:   22 MacArtain, P., Gill, C.I.R., Brooks, M., Campbell, R. and Rowland, I.R. (2007). Nutritional value of edible seaweeds. *Nutrition Review*, 65 (12), pp. 535-543. Also: McCance, R.A., Widdowson, E.M. and Holland, B. (1993). *McCance and Widdowson's The composition of foods.* 6th edition. Cambridge: Royal Society of Chemistry.

NOTES

Table 4. Mineral composition of seaweeds compared to whole foods

Food Type	Calcium	Potassium	Magnesium	Sodium	Copper	Iron	Iodine	Zinc
Seaweed								
(mg/100g wet weight)*								
Ascophyllum nodosum	575.0	765.0	225.0	1173.8	0.8	14.9	18.2	NA
Laminaria digitata	364.7	2013.2	403.5	624.6	0.3	45.6	70.0	1.6
Himanthalia elongata	30.0	1351.4	90.1	600.6	0.1	5.0	10.7	1.7
Undaria pinnatifida	112.3	62.4	78.7	448.7	0.2	3.9	3.9	0.3
Porphyra umbilicalis	34.2	302.2	108.3	1199.7	0.1	5.2	1.3	0.7
Palmaria palmata	148.8	1169.6	97.6	255.2	0.4	12.8	10.2	0.3
Chondrus crispus	373.8	827.5	573.8	1572.5	0.1	6.6	6.1	NA
Ulva spp.	325.0	245.0	465.0	340.0	0.3	15.3	1.6	0.9
Enteromorpha spp.	104.0	351.1	455.1	52.0	0.1	22.2	97.9	1.2
Whole food								
(mg/100g weight)†								
Brown rice	110.0	1160.0	520.0	28.0	1.3	12.9	NA	16.2
Whole milk	115.0	140.0	11.0	55.0	Tr	0.1	15.0	0.4
Cheddar cheese	720.0	77.0	25.0	670.0	0.0	0.3	39.0	2.3
Sirloin steak	9.0	260.0	16.0	49.0	0.1	1.6	6.0	3.1
Lentils green and brown	71.0	940.0	110.0	12.0	1.0	11.1	NA	3.9
Spinach	170.0	500.0	54.0	140.0	0.0	2.1	2.0	0.7
Bananas	6.0	400.0	34.0	1.0	0.1	0.3	8.0	0.2
Brazil nut	170.0	660.0	410.0	3.0	1.8	2.5	20.0	4.2
Peanuts	60.0	670.0	210.0	2.0	1.0	2.5	20.0	3.5

Mineral composition of seaweeds compared to whole foods *Nutrition Review*, Vol. 65, No. 12.

Values for seaweed from the Institut de Phytonutrition (2004)

Values for whole foods from McCance et al. (1993)

INDEX

The main page reference for each seaweed is indicated in bold

INDEX